MAYER SMITH

The Court of Endless Dusk

This book was professionally typeset on Reedsy.
Find out more at reedsy.com

Contents

One

Shadows of a Forgotten Realm

The village of Greystone was perched on the edge of the world, or so it seemed. Thick forests of ashwood bordered it on one side, and on the other, the Vale of Dusk—a place of whispered legends—stretched into the horizon, veiled in a perpetual twilight. For the people of Greystone, life was simple, almost ritualistic. They lived by the rhythm of the seasons, tending to their crops, mending their homes, and whispering prayers to ward off whatever lingered beyond the misty borders of the Vale.

Evanna sat by the hearth in her modest cottage, her nimble fingers weaving dried herbs into garlands. The scent of lavender and sage mingled with the faint tang of burning wood, wrapping the room in a sense of calm. Her dark hair was pulled back in a loose braid, and her green eyes glimmered with determination as she worked. Healing was her gift, her duty—

a responsibility she had carried since her mother's untimely death years ago. The villagers relied on her, not only for medicine but also for protection from the unseen dangers that seemed to seep into their lives like an invasive vine.

As the last of the garlands was hung to dry, a loud knock echoed through the room, startling her. Evanna's heart leapt to her throat as she turned to the door. No one knocked like that—not in the middle of the night. She hesitated, her gaze darting to the dagger resting on the mantel.

Another knock came, more urgent this time.

"Who's there?" she called, her voice steady despite the knot of unease tightening in her chest.

For a moment, there was no answer. Then, a voice—low and strained—came through the heavy oak door. "Help me… please."

Evanna hesitated. She wasn't naïve. The Vale's shadowy tendrils were said to reach out to the unwary, luring them into its grasp. But the voice sounded human, desperate. Against her better judgment, she grabbed the dagger and opened the door a crack.

A man stumbled into the doorway, clutching his side. His dark hair was matted with sweat, and his clothes were torn and bloodied. Evanna barely had time to react before he collapsed at her feet.

She dropped to her knees, instinct taking over as she checked for signs of life. His breathing was shallow, his pulse weak but present. She caught sight of strange markings on his forearm, intricate and swirling like ancient runes. A shiver ran down her spine, but there was no time for hesitation.

Dragging the man inside, she laid him on her worktable, which was strewn with herbs and vials. The firelight illuminated his pale face, sharp features marred by exhaustion. His hands twitched slightly as if clutching at something unseen.

"Who are you?" she whispered, more to herself than to him.

The man's eyes fluttered open briefly, their piercing blue gaze locking onto hers. "Don't… let them… find me," he rasped before slipping into unconsciousness.

—-

The hours stretched into the early morning as Evanna worked tirelessly. She cleaned and stitched the gash on his side, her hands steady despite the growing sense of unease. There was something otherworldly about him, something that didn't belong in her quiet village.

As dawn broke, she sat back, exhaustion weighing on her like a stone. The man's breathing had steadied, and the color had returned to his cheeks. She studied his markings again, brushing her fingers lightly over the strange symbols. They seemed to shimmer faintly in the dim light, as though alive.

A sudden knock at the door jolted her. This one was different—firm, authoritative. She rose quickly, her heart pounding in her ears. Through the narrow window, she caught sight of three figures dressed in dark cloaks, their faces obscured by hoods.

"Open the door," one of them commanded, his voice cold and sharp like a blade.

Evanna's instincts screamed at her to stay silent, but the sound of footsteps approaching the window told her she didn't have much time. She glanced at the man on the table, her mind racing. Whoever these people were, they were clearly after him—and she didn't trust them.

Grabbing a blanket, she threw it over the man to conceal him and then moved to the door, cracking it open just enough to meet the intruders' gaze.

"What do you want?" she asked, her voice steady despite the hammering in her chest.

"We're looking for someone," the leader said, his hood tilting as if to peer past her. "A man—wounded, dangerous. Have you seen him?"

"No," she lied, her fingers tightening around the edge of the door.

The man leaned closer, his presence suffocating. "You would do well not to lie to us, healer. The Court of Endless Dusk does not take kindly to deception."

The name sent a chill through her. The Court of Endless Dusk was a myth, a story told to frighten children into obedience. Yet, standing before these strangers, she felt the weight of something ancient and sinister pressing down on her.

"I don't know what you're talking about," she said firmly, meeting his gaze.

The man studied her for a moment longer, then stepped back. "If you see him, remember—there are worse fates than death."

Without another word, the trio disappeared into the mist, their figures dissolving like shadows under the rising sun.

—-

Evanna locked the door and leaned against it, her breath coming in shallow gasps. She turned to find the man on the table awake, his eyes filled with a mixture of fear and gratitude.

"You… lied for me," he said hoarsely.

"I don't know who you are or what you've done," she replied, her voice sharper than she intended. "But you brought danger to my home, and I need answers."

The man sat up with a wince, his hand instinctively covering the stitched wound. "My name is Callen," he said after a pause. "I… don't remember much, but I know I can't let them take me. They're from the Court. If they find me, it's over—for all of us."

"What is the Court of Endless Dusk?" Evanna demanded.

Callen hesitated, his gaze darting to the window as if expecting the cloaked figures to return. "It's a place of power, of shadows. The Queen… she rules it. And I…" He trailed off, his expression haunted.

"You what?"

"I think I betrayed her."

Evanna's blood ran cold. Whatever Callen was mixed up in, it was far beyond anything she had ever encountered. But the thought of turning him away felt impossible. The fear in his eyes was real, and beneath it was a desperation that mirrored her own loneliness.

As the first rays of sunlight filtered through the window, Evanna made a silent decision. Whatever the cost, she would uncover the truth—about Callen, the Court of Endless Dusk, and the shadows that had begun to creep into her quiet life.

In that moment, she realized the boundaries of her world were about to shatter. And there would be no going back.

Two

The Mark of the Court

The morning mist clung stubbornly to the village of Greystone, wrapping every house and cobbled path in a shroud of secrecy. Evanna paced the length of her modest cottage, her thoughts tumbling over each other like a stormy sea. On her worktable, Callen sat propped against the wall, his skin pale but his gaze sharp. His disheveled dark hair cast shadows over his piercing blue eyes, which darted to every corner of the room as if expecting danger to leap from the very walls.

Evanna stopped pacing and faced him, her arms crossed tightly over her chest. "You have to tell me everything. Who are those people? What is this Court? And what do these marks mean?" She gestured toward the swirling patterns etched into his forearm.

Callen hesitated, running a hand through his hair as though trying to pull an answer from the depths of his mind. "I told you last night—I don't remember everything," he said, his voice strained. "But I know enough to say this: those men are hunters. They serve the Queen of Endless Dusk, and their only purpose is to find me and take me back."

"Back where?" Evanna demanded.

"To the Court," he said, his tone darkening. "It's not a place you want to imagine, let alone step into. The Queen rules over shadows, fear, and secrets. And once you're in her grasp, you don't escape."

Evanna narrowed her eyes, her skepticism hardening her features. "That doesn't explain why they're after you—or why you have those marks. Are you one of them?"

Callen flinched at her words, his gaze dropping to the intricate symbols spiraling across his skin. "No. At least… I don't think I am." His fingers brushed over the markings, his expression a mixture of fear and loathing. "These… these aren't natural. They're a brand, a claim. The Queen's magic leaves its mark on those she binds to her will."

Evanna's breath caught, her mind racing. She had seen strange things in her time as the village healer—unexplained fevers, unnatural shadows creeping at the edge of the Vale—but nothing like this. "So you're bound to her? Is that what you're saying?"

"I don't know," Callen said, frustration seeping into his voice. "I remember running, fleeing the Court. I remember defying her, something no one does and lives to tell about. But how I got here, or why… it's like trying to hold water in my hands."

—-

The room fell into an uneasy silence, broken only by the distant sound of a crow cawing. Evanna's eyes lingered on the markings, an odd shimmer catching her attention as the light shifted. Tentatively, she reached out and touched one of the swirling patterns.

The instant her fingers made contact, a surge of cold shot up her arm, and her vision blurred. For a brief moment, she wasn't in her cottage anymore. Instead, she stood in a dark, endless expanse, where faint whispers curled around her like smoke. A pale figure with glowing eyes loomed ahead, and the overwhelming sense of being watched pressed down on her chest like a heavy weight.

"Evanna!" Callen's voice yanked her back to reality. She stumbled, clutching the edge of the table for support.

"What just happened?" she asked, her voice shaking.

Callen's face was pale, his own hands trembling. "You touched the mark," he said, his tone edged with panic. "No one's supposed to do that—it connects you to her."

"Her?"

"The Queen," he said grimly. "If she felt you… if she knows you're helping me…" He trailed off, his gaze darting toward the door as if expecting it to burst open at any moment.

—-

Before Evanna could respond, another knock shattered the tension in the room. This time, it was softer but no less insistent. Her heart raced as she exchanged a glance with Callen.

"Stay hidden," she whispered, motioning for him to duck behind a shelf laden with herbs and jars.

With a deep breath, she opened the door to find Elder Alric, the village's leader and keeper of its stories. His hunched frame leaned heavily on a carved staff, and his gray eyes were sharp with suspicion.

"Good morning, Elder," Evanna said, trying to mask the tremor in her voice.

"Morning, child," Alric replied, his tone grave. "There are troubling whispers in the village. Strangers in dark cloaks were seen near your home last night. I came to make sure all is well."

Evanna hesitated, the weight of the truth pressing heavily on her tongue. "I'm fine," she said carefully. "No strangers here."

Alric studied her for a long moment, his gaze piercing. "You would tell me if there were, wouldn't you? The Vale's shadows have a way of seeping into places they don't belong. We cannot risk inviting danger into our midst."

"I understand, Elder," she said, forcing a smile. "I promise, everything is fine."

He nodded slowly, though his expression remained skeptical. "Be cautious, Evanna. Shadows have a way of hiding in plain sight."

With that, he turned and hobbled away, his staff clicking against the cobblestones. Evanna closed the door, leaning against it as she exhaled shakily.

—-

"That was close," Callen muttered, emerging from his hiding spot.

Evanna rounded on him, her frustration bubbling over. "Close doesn't even begin to cover it. Do you have any idea what kind of danger you've brought here? If the villagers find out, they'll turn you over to those hunters without a second thought."

"I didn't ask for your help," Callen shot back, his voice sharp. "You could've left me out there to die."

"I should have," she snapped, but the words rang hollow in her ears. She knew she couldn't have ignored his plea, no matter the danger it brought.

The tension between them hung heavy in the air until Callen broke it with a weary sigh. "I'm sorry," he said quietly. "I don't want to drag you into this, but… I don't think I can do it alone."

Evanna studied him, the vulnerability in his eyes softening her anger. Despite her fear and frustration, she couldn't shake the feeling that helping him was the right thing to do.

"We need answers," she said finally. "If we're going to figure out what's happening, we'll need to start at the source."

Callen's brow furrowed. "The source?"

"The Vale," she said, her voice steady. "If the Court is connected to it, then that's where we'll find our answers."

Callen's face darkened, his jaw tightening. "The Vale is dangerous. No one comes back from it."

"Then it's a good thing I'm not easily scared," Evanna replied, surprising even herself with the determination in her tone.

For a moment, Callen just stared at her, as though seeing her for the first time. Then he nodded, a flicker of hope lighting his features. "All right," he said. "But we'll need to move quickly. The hunters won't stop until they find me."

As Evanna gathered supplies, a chill ran through her. The Vale of Dusk loomed in the distance, its misty borders hiding secrets far older than her village. For the first time, she wondered if she was truly prepared for the journey ahead—or the shadows it would reveal.

Three

Whispered Warnings

The trek toward the Vale of Dusk began in the cold embrace of dawn. The sun struggled to pierce through the thick blanket of mist that clung to the village outskirts, casting long shadows that seemed to stretch unnaturally across the path. Evanna tightened the straps on her satchel, her fingers trembling slightly as she checked its contents: herbs, poultices, and a small, sharpened blade. Practical tools, yet they felt insufficient for the weight of the journey ahead.

Callen walked beside her, his gait unsteady but determined. The bandages around his torso were fresh, though the strain on his face revealed he was still in pain. Despite this, he moved with a quiet resolve, his piercing blue eyes scanning the dense forest ahead.

"You're sure about this?" Evanna asked, breaking the uneasy silence.

"No," he admitted. "But we don't have much of a choice."

The path narrowed as they entered the forest, the trees pressing in around them. The air grew cooler, and the chirping of birds faded into an eerie silence. It was as if the forest itself held its breath, watching their every step.

As they walked, Callen's hand unconsciously drifted to the markings on his forearm. Evanna noticed but said nothing, though her curiosity gnawed at her. The marks seemed almost alive, faintly glowing whenever the shadows deepened.

"Does it hurt?" she finally asked.

Callen glanced at her, then back at his arm. "Not exactly," he said. "It's more like… a pull. Like it's trying to lead me somewhere."

"Lead you where?"

He hesitated, his jaw tightening. "To her."

Evanna swallowed hard, the weight of his words sinking in. She glanced over her shoulder, half expecting to see cloaked figures emerging from the mist. "We need to be careful," she said, her voice low. "Those hunters might still be nearby."

Callen nodded, his expression grim. "They won't stop until

they find me. Or until I'm dead."

—-

Hours passed, the dense forest blurring into an endless expanse of gray and green. The only sounds were the crunch of leaves beneath their boots and the occasional snap of a branch. Evanna's nerves were fraying with every step, her senses on high alert.

It was late afternoon when they came upon a small clearing. At its center stood a weathered stone monument, its surface etched with faded symbols that bore a striking resemblance to the markings on Callen's arm.

"This wasn't on the map," Evanna murmured, approaching the monument cautiously.

Callen followed, his gaze fixed on the stone. "It feels… familiar," he said, running his fingers over the carvings.

As his hand touched the stone, a sudden chill swept through the clearing. The air seemed to hum with an unseen energy, and the forest grew unnaturally still. Evanna took a step back, her heart pounding.

"Callen, stop," she urged, but it was too late.

The carvings began to glow, their light a deep, pulsating blue. The hum grew louder, transforming into a cacophony of whispers that seemed to come from everywhere and nowhere all at once.

Evanna clapped her hands over her ears, her knees buckling under the weight of the sound. "What's happening?" she shouted, but her voice was drowned out by the whispers.

Callen stood frozen, his eyes wide with a mixture of awe and terror. The light from the stone spread, crawling up his arm and igniting the markings on his skin. He let out a strangled cry, collapsing to the ground as the whispers reached a deafening crescendo.

And then, just as suddenly as it began, the light and sound vanished. The clearing was plunged into silence once more.

Evanna scrambled to Callen's side, her hands shaking as she checked for signs of life. His breathing was shallow, but his pulse was steady. She shook him gently. "Callen, wake up!"

His eyes fluttered open, and for a moment, they glowed with the same eerie blue light. "She's coming," he rasped.

"Who?" Evanna demanded.

But before he could answer, a deep voice spoke from the shadows. "You should not have touched the stone."

Evanna spun around, her dagger in hand. A figure emerged from the treeline—a tall, wiry man clad in tattered robes, his face obscured by a hood. His presence exuded an unsettling combination of wisdom and menace.

"Who are you?" she asked, her voice steady despite the fear coursing through her veins.

The man stepped closer, his movements slow and deliberate. "I am Malric," he said, his tone calm but laced with warning. "Keeper of this place. And you, foolish children, have awakened forces you cannot begin to understand."

"We didn't mean to," Evanna said quickly, placing herself between Malric and Callen. "We're just passing through."

Malric's gaze shifted to Callen, his eyes narrowing. "The mark on his arm says otherwise. He is bound to the Queen. She will sense his presence now, and she will come for him."

Callen struggled to sit up, his voice weak but defiant. "I won't go back," he said. "I'd rather die."

Malric let out a low chuckle, though there was no humor in it. "You may find death preferable to what awaits you if she finds you. The Queen of Endless Dusk does not forgive betrayal."

Evanna clenched her fists, her frustration bubbling over. "Then tell us how to stop her! There must be a way to break her hold."

Malric studied her for a long moment, then sighed heavily. "There is no breaking her hold," he said. "Not entirely. But there are ways to resist, to delay. You must travel to the heart of the Vale and seek the Shrine of Shadows. There, you may find the answers you seek."

"The Shrine of Shadows?" Callen repeated, his brow furrowing.

"It is a place of great power," Malric said. "But it is also a place of great peril. Many who seek it do not return."

Evanna exchanged a glance with Callen, her resolve hardening. "Then we'll go," she said firmly. "We've come this far. We can't turn back now."

Malric's expression softened, a hint of pity flickering in his eyes. "Bravery will only carry you so far, child," he said. "Beware the shadows, and trust no one—not even each other."

Before Evanna could respond, Malric turned and disappeared into the forest, his form swallowed by the mist.

—-

The clearing was silent once more, but the weight of Malric's warning lingered in the air.

"We should rest," Evanna said, helping Callen to his feet. "We'll need all our strength for what's ahead."

Callen nodded, though his expression was distant. As they set up a small camp at the edge of the clearing, Evanna couldn't shake the feeling that they were being watched.

The forest around them seemed to close in, the shadows growing darker with each passing moment. She glanced at Callen, who was staring at the glowing markings on his arm.

For the first time, Evanna wondered if Malric's final words held more truth than she cared to admit.

"Trust no one," she murmured to herself, her gaze lingering on Callen.

The words echoed in her mind as the last light of day faded, leaving them in the eerie embrace of the Court's shadowy reach.

Four

Journey into the Unknown

The Vale of Dusk loomed before them like a living shadow, its swirling mists curling around the gnarled trunks of ancient trees. The boundary between the world they knew and the one they feared was marked by a jagged black stone archway covered in moss and creeping vines. The air here was colder, heavier, carrying a faint metallic tang that prickled against the skin. Evanna hesitated at the threshold, her heart pounding in her chest as though it sought to warn her of the danger that lay ahead.

Beside her, Callen adjusted the straps of his satchel, his movements stiff with tension. His gaze remained fixed on the archway, where the mist shifted as if alive, beckoning them forward. The markings on his forearm glowed faintly, pulsing in rhythm with his heartbeat.

"Once we cross, there's no turning back," Callen said, his voice low but steady.

Evanna nodded, gripping the hilt of the dagger strapped to her belt. "We've come this far. We can't stop now."

The two exchanged a brief glance, their unspoken resolve binding them together. With a deep breath, they stepped through the archway and into the Vale.

—-

The change was immediate and unsettling. The light dimmed, replaced by a pale, silvery glow that seemed to emanate from the mist itself. The air grew thicker, carrying with it a faint whispering that was just loud enough to unsettle the senses but too quiet to decipher. Every sound they made—the crunch of leaves beneath their boots, the rustle of their packs—felt amplified, as though the Vale were listening.

Evanna tightened her grip on her dagger, her eyes scanning their surroundings. The trees here were unlike any she had seen before, their trunks twisted and blackened as though scorched by fire. Their branches reached out like skeletal hands, draped in ghostly gray moss that swayed despite the still air.

"It feels… wrong," she murmured.

Callen's gaze darted around the forest, his expression tense. "The Vale isn't like the world outside. It bends and shifts, reacting to your thoughts, your fears. You have to stay focused, or it will consume you."

Evanna shivered, but she nodded. "Lead the way."

—-

Hours passed, though it was impossible to tell time in the unchanging twilight of the Vale. The forest seemed to stretch endlessly, each twist and turn of the path leading them deeper into the unknown. Every so often, the whispers grew louder, their tone more insistent.

"What are they saying?" Evanna asked, her voice barely above a whisper.

"They're not saying anything," Callen replied, his jaw tight. "They're testing you. Trying to find a weakness they can exploit."

Evanna swallowed hard, her eyes flickering to the shadows that seemed to dance at the edges of her vision. She could almost swear she saw figures there—vague, humanoid shapes that vanished the moment she turned to look at them.

"Don't let them get to you," Callen warned, his voice sharp. "They're not real."

But Evanna wasn't so sure.

—-

The first true challenge came as they approached a wide, dark river. The water was unnaturally still, its surface reflecting the silvery light of the mist. A single, narrow bridge of crumbling stone spanned the river, its edges worn and uneven.

"This doesn't feel safe," Evanna said, eyeing the bridge warily.

"It's not," Callen said. "But we don't have another option."

As they stepped onto the bridge, the whispers intensified, rising to a deafening chorus that seemed to come from the river itself. Evanna froze, her hands flying to her ears.

"Keep moving!" Callen shouted over the noise, his voice barely audible.

Evanna forced herself to take another step, her legs trembling. The whispers grew louder, morphing into voices—familiar voices.

"Why didn't you save me?" a voice hissed, cold and accusatory.

Evanna's blood ran cold. "Mother?" she whispered, her eyes darting to the water below.

In the river's surface, she saw a reflection of her mother's face, pale and gaunt, her eyes filled with pain. The image reached out, its lips moving in a silent scream.

"It's not real!" Callen shouted, grabbing her arm and pulling her forward.

The contact broke the spell, and Evanna stumbled across the bridge, her heart racing. She didn't look back.

—-

By the time they reached the other side, both were breathing heavily, their nerves frayed. Evanna leaned against a tree, her hands shaking.

"What was that?" she demanded, her voice trembling.

"The Vale feeds on your guilt," Callen said, his tone grim. "It pulls your darkest thoughts to the surface and makes you face them."

Evanna stared at him, her mind reeling. "You've been through this before, haven't you?"

Callen hesitated, then nodded. "When I first escaped the Court. The Vale tried to break me then, too."

"And did it?"

Callen didn't answer.

—-

As they pressed on, the forest grew darker, the shadows deeper. The air grew colder, and a sense of unease settled over them like a heavy blanket.

It was Evanna who noticed the change first. "Do you hear that?" she asked, stopping in her tracks.

Callen frowned, straining to listen. At first, there was only silence. Then, faintly, the sound of footsteps echoed through the forest.

"They're not ours," Evanna whispered, her hand tightening around her dagger.

The footsteps grew louder, more deliberate. They were not alone.

"Stay close," Callen said, drawing a small, curved blade from his belt.

The two moved cautiously, their eyes scanning the forest for any sign of movement. The footsteps stopped abruptly, replaced by a low, guttural growl.

Evanna's breath caught as a pair of glowing yellow eyes appeared in the darkness. Then another. And another.

Wolves, but not like any wolves she had ever seen. Their fur was matted and dark, their bodies unnaturally large. They moved with an eerie, jerky grace, their eyes fixed on the intruders.

"Run," Callen said, his voice barely above a whisper.

Evanna didn't need to be told twice. She bolted, the wolves' growls turning into deafening snarls as they gave chase.

The forest blurred around her as she ran, her heart pounding in her chest. She could hear Callen behind her, his footsteps quick and steady.

"Left!" he shouted, and she veered off the path, narrowly avoiding one of the wolves as it lunged at her.

The trees seemed to close in around them, their branches clawing at her skin. The snarls grew louder, closer. Evanna's lungs burned, her legs screaming in protest, but she didn't dare slow down.

Ahead, the forest opened up into another clearing, and in its center stood a massive stone obelisk. The markings on it glowed faintly, pulsing in time with the whispers that filled the air.

"Get to the obelisk!" Callen shouted, his voice filled with urgency.

Evanna stumbled into the clearing, her eyes locked on the obelisk. As she reached out to touch it, a blinding light erupted from its surface, accompanied by a wave of energy that knocked her to the ground.

The wolves yelped and retreated, their forms dissolving into the mist as quickly as they had appeared.

Evanna lay on the ground, gasping for breath, her body trembling. Callen knelt beside her, his expression a mixture of relief and concern.

"You're okay," he said, his voice soothing. "We're safe. For now."

Evanna nodded weakly, her mind racing. The Vale was testing them at every turn, pushing them closer to the edge. And this was only the beginning.

As she stared up at the glowing obelisk, one thought echoed in her mind: What horrors lay ahead in the heart of the Vale?

Five

The Gatekeeper's Riddle

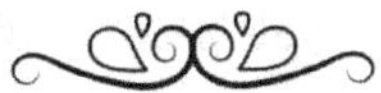

The obelisk stood like a silent sentinel in the center of the clearing, its surface etched with swirling patterns that glowed faintly in the dim light of the Vale. Evanna's fingers traced the cool stone, her heart still racing from the wolf encounter. The glow pulsed in rhythm with her heartbeat, almost as if the obelisk were alive, reacting to her presence.

"We can't stay here long," Callen said, his voice low and urgent. He stood a few steps behind her, his blade still in hand, scanning the treeline for any signs of danger. "The light might have scared off the wolves, but it's also a beacon. Something else might come."

Evanna nodded, though her gaze remained fixed on the obelisk. There was something unsettlingly familiar about the markings, as though she had seen them before in dreams or fragments of forgotten memories.

"What is this place?" she asked, her voice barely above a whisper.

Callen stepped closer, his expression grim. "A waypoint," he said. "The Court uses these to mark paths through the Vale. They're ancient, tied to the Queen's power. They're supposed to guide those who are loyal to her—or test those who aren't."

Evanna's stomach twisted. "Test how?"

Before Callen could answer, the light from the obelisk flared, blinding and intense. Evanna shielded her eyes, staggering back as the clearing was bathed in an ethereal glow. When the light dimmed, a figure stood before them.

The Gatekeeper.

It was neither man nor woman but something in between, its form cloaked in flowing silver robes that seemed to shimmer and shift like liquid. Its face was obscured by a featureless mask, smooth and pale, with two hollow voids where eyes should have been. It carried an air of authority, its presence oppressive and commanding.

"Travelers," the Gatekeeper intoned, its voice echoing unnaturally as if it came from everywhere at once. "You seek passage through the Vale of Dusk. But the way forward is not freely given. You must earn it."

Evanna's throat went dry. "Who are you?"

"I am the Keeper of this path," the figure replied. "A servant of the Queen, bound to her will. Those who tread this land must prove their worth, lest they fall prey to the shadows."

Callen stepped forward, his jaw set. "We don't serve the Queen. We're not here to harm the Vale."

The Gatekeeper tilted its head, as though considering his words. "You bear her mark," it said, gesturing toward Callen's glowing forearm. "And yet you defy her. A contradiction. You intrigue me, Wanderer."

Callen stiffened but said nothing.

The Gatekeeper's hollow gaze turned to Evanna. "And you, healer. Your presence here is an anomaly. The Queen has no claim on you, yet you walk willingly into her domain. Why?"

Evanna met its gaze—or what she assumed was its gaze. "Because I want answers. About the Vale. About the Court. About him." She nodded toward Callen.

The Gatekeeper regarded her for a long moment, then nodded slowly. "Then you shall have the chance to earn them. But first, you must face my riddle."

—-

The Gatekeeper raised a hand, and the air around them shifted.

The clearing darkened, and the obelisk's light dimmed to a faint glow. The trees at the edges of the clearing twisted and writhed, their branches intertwining to form an impenetrable barrier. Evanna's breath hitched as the space seemed to close in around them.

"You will answer my riddle," the Gatekeeper said. "Three attempts you shall have. Fail, and the shadows will claim you. Succeed, and the path will open."

Evanna's heart pounded in her chest, but she nodded. "We're ready."

The Gatekeeper's voice deepened, resonating with a power that made the ground tremble beneath their feet.

"I am not alive, yet I grow.
    I do not have lungs, yet I need air.
    I do not have a mouth, yet I can drown.
    What am I?"

—-

The riddle hung in the air like a heavy weight. Evanna's mind raced, her thoughts colliding in a frantic attempt to make sense of the cryptic words. She glanced at Callen, who was frowning in concentration.

"Not alive, yet it grows," she murmured. "No lungs, but it needs air. No mouth, but it can drown…"

"Fire," Callen said suddenly, his voice firm.

Evanna looked at him, her eyes widening. "What?"

"It's fire," he repeated. "Fire grows, but it's not alive. It needs air to survive, and it's extinguished by water."

Evanna turned back to the Gatekeeper. "Fire. The answer is fire."

The Gatekeeper tilted its head, its featureless mask unreadable. For a moment, the clearing was silent. Then the figure nodded.

"Correct," it said, its voice echoing with approval. "The first trial is passed. Two remain."

—-

The Gatekeeper raised its hand again, and the air grew colder. The whispers that had lingered on the edges of the clearing grew louder, more insistent, until they became words. Evanna froze as she recognized the voice—her mother's voice.

"Evanna," the whisper said, soft and pleading. "Why didn't you save me?"

Her vision blurred, and for a moment, she was back in the cottage where her mother had drawn her final breath, her hand clutching Evanna's. The memory hit her like a physical blow, and she staggered, her knees threatening to buckle.

"It's not real!" Callen's voice cut through the illusion, grounding her. "It's another test!"

Evanna forced herself to focus, the clearing coming back into view. The Gatekeeper stood motionless, waiting.

"Your second trial is one of truth," it said. "You must reveal that which you hide, even from yourself."

Evanna's breath caught, and her gaze darted to Callen. She wanted to protest, to refuse, but the Gatekeeper's presence left no room for argument.

"I…" Her voice faltered.

Callen placed a steadying hand on her shoulder. "It's okay," he said quietly.

Evanna closed her eyes, forcing the words out. "I blame myself. For my mother's death. I was too afraid to take her place, to do what she asked of me. And because of that, she died."

The confession tore through her, leaving her raw and exposed. Tears streamed down her face, but the whispers faded, and the cold air warmed slightly.

The Gatekeeper nodded. "Truth is the key to the second trial. You have passed."

—-

The clearing shifted again, the trees retreating slightly to reveal a faint path beyond the obelisk.

"Your final trial lies ahead," the Gatekeeper said. "You must face the shadows and let them see you. Only then will the way forward be revealed."

Before Evanna or Callen could respond, the figure vanished, leaving them alone in the eerie stillness.

—-

Evanna wiped her eyes, her body trembling from the weight of the trials. Callen squeezed her shoulder gently, his expression unreadable.

"We're close," he said, his voice steady. "One more step, and we'll be through."

Evanna nodded, though her fear lingered. As they stepped onto the path, the shadows seemed to gather around them, their whispers growing louder. She gripped her dagger tightly, her resolve hardening.

No matter what lay ahead, she would face it.

For the answers. For Callen.

And for herself.

Six

The Court of Echoes

The path beyond the obelisk was narrow and twisting, lined with jagged rocks and dense foliage that seemed to shift and writhe in the corner of Evanna's vision. The whispers from the Gatekeeper's trials still clung to her ears like an unwelcome melody, their words taunting her with fragments of her fears and regrets. The air in the Vale grew colder as they ventured deeper, the oppressive silence broken only by the crunch of their boots on the uneven ground.

Callen walked ahead, his blade still in hand, the faint glow of the markings on his arm casting eerie shadows against the trees. Evanna followed closely, her senses heightened and her heart pounding with every step. The path felt alive, as if it were watching them, guiding them toward something unknown and inescapable.

"How far do you think this goes?" Evanna asked, her voice barely above a whisper.

Callen glanced back at her, his expression grim. "Far enough that most don't come back."

"That's not comforting."

"It wasn't meant to be."

Evanna rolled her eyes, though her unease lingered. The path opened into a clearing, and they both stopped in their tracks. Before them stood a vast expanse of ruins, their edges softened by time and overgrowth. The structures were angular and alien, made of a dark, iridescent stone that seemed to hum faintly with energy. Columns rose like skeletal fingers toward the sky, and shattered archways marked the remnants of once-grand halls.

At the center of the ruins was a towering spire, its surface covered in the same swirling markings that adorned Callen's arm. A faint light emanated from the top, casting long, shifting shadows across the ground.

"The Court of Echoes," Callen said, his voice tinged with awe and dread.

—-

As they stepped into the ruins, the whispers returned, louder and more insistent than before. They were no longer just faint murmurs but fully formed voices, each distinct yet overlapping in a chaotic symphony. Evanna paused, her head swiveling as the voices seemed to come from every direction.

"Evanna…"

The sound of her name sent a chill down her spine. She turned sharply, her dagger raised, but there was no one there.

"They know us," she whispered, her voice trembling.

"They know you," Callen corrected, his eyes scanning the ruins. "The Court has always been drawn to guilt, to secrets. The voices reflect what we've buried." He glanced at her, his expression unreadable. "Be careful what you listen to."

Evanna nodded, though her heart was already racing. The ruins felt alive, each shadow and echo conspiring to unravel her resolve. As they moved deeper into the Court, the voices grew louder, their tones shifting from pleading to mocking.

"You failed her," one voice hissed, low and venomous.

"She would have lived if not for you," another sneered.

Evanna clenched her fists, willing herself to ignore the voices. But with each step, the weight of their words pressed harder against her chest.

—-

They approached the base of the spire, where an enormous double door stood slightly ajar. Intricate carvings covered its surface, depicting scenes of a queen seated on a throne, her subjects kneeling before her. The figures were faceless, their forms distorted as if they were dissolving into shadows.

Callen hesitated, his hand hovering near the door. "Once we go in, we'll be fully in the Court's domain. There's no telling what we'll find."

"We didn't come this far to turn back," Evanna said, though her voice wavered.

Callen nodded and pushed the door open with a groan of ancient hinges. The air inside was colder, heavier, as though the space itself was alive and breathing. The room they entered was vast and circular, its walls lined with towering mirrors. Each mirror reflected not their current surroundings but fragmented, distorted images that shifted and changed as they moved.

"What is this place?" Evanna asked, her voice hushed.

"The Hall of Reflections," Callen said. "A test, like the others. The mirrors show you things—truths, lies, memories. You can't trust what you see."

Evanna approached one of the mirrors cautiously, her breath catching as the surface rippled like water. Her reflection stared back at her, but it wasn't quite right. The woman in the mirror looked older, her face lined with sorrow and regret. Her green eyes were hollow, and her hands trembled as though burdened by an unseen weight.

"You're not strong enough," the reflection whispered, its voice tinged with venom. "You never were."

Evanna stumbled back, her pulse quickening. She turned to Callen, who stood before another mirror, his jaw clenched and his hands balled into fists.

"What do you see?" she asked, her voice shaking.

Callen didn't answer. His gaze remained locked on the mirror, his face pale. After a long moment, he reached out, his fingers brushing the surface. The mirror rippled, and a scene unfolded within its depths.

A grand throne room appeared, its walls lined with shadowy figures. At the center sat a woman with piercing golden eyes and a crown of twisting black thorns. She radiated power, her presence overwhelming even through the reflection. At her feet knelt a younger version of Callen, his head bowed.

"You will serve me," the Queen said, her voice smooth and commanding. "You have no choice."

Callen in the reflection looked up, his eyes filled with both fear and defiance. "I'll never serve you."

The Queen smiled, a cold and calculating expression. "Oh, but you already do."

The image dissolved, and Callen stumbled back, his breathing ragged. "We need to keep moving," he said, his voice tight.

Evanna hesitated, but the urgency in his tone spurred her forward. Together, they moved through the Hall, the mirrors whispering and shifting as they passed. The voices grew louder, more insistent, until they reached a door at the far end of the room.

—-

The door opened into a smaller chamber, its walls covered in the same swirling markings as the obelisk and the spire. At the center of the room was a pedestal, and atop it rested a black crystal that pulsed with a faint, malevolent light.

"The Heart of the Court," Callen said, his voice reverent and fearful. "This is what she uses to bind her power."

Evanna stepped closer, her hand hovering near the crystal. The whispers in the room intensified, filling her mind with fragments of thoughts that weren't her own.

"Take it," one voice urged. "Use it against her."

"Destroy it," another countered. "End her reign."

"Leave it," a third warned. "It will consume you."

Evanna's hand trembled as she reached for the crystal. She could feel its power, cold and sharp, like a blade pressed against her skin.

"Don't touch it," Callen said, his voice cutting through the chaos. "The Heart is dangerous. If you take it, you'll be tied to the Court forever."

Evanna hesitated, the weight of the decision pressing down on her. But before she could decide, the shadows in the room shifted, and the whispers coalesced into a single, chilling voice.

"You should not be here."

The Queen.

Her presence filled the chamber, a shadowy figure with glowing golden eyes that pierced through the darkness. Evanna froze, her heart hammering in her chest as the Queen's gaze locked onto her.

"You dare to trespass in my domain?" the Queen said, her voice smooth and deadly. "You will pay the price."

Before either of them could react, the shadows surged forward, engulfing the room in darkness. Evanna's scream was swallowed by the void as she felt herself pulled into the endless, suffocating embrace of the Court.

And then, there was silence.

Seven

The Queen's Champion

Darkness surrounded Evanna like a shroud, pressing against her from all sides. She could feel its weight, cold and suffocating, as though it were alive and intent on consuming her whole. Her breaths came in shallow gasps, her heart pounding as she strained to find any sense of direction. The whispers of the Court were gone, replaced by an eerie silence that was somehow more unnerving.

"Callen?" she called, her voice barely a whisper.

There was no answer. She reached out blindly, her fingers brushing against nothing but air. Panic began to creep into her chest, her mind racing with the fear that she was alone—truly alone—in this desolate void.

Then, a faint light appeared in the distance. It was dim and flickering, but it pierced through the darkness like a beacon. Evanna hesitated for a moment, then moved toward it, her steps cautious and unsteady. The ground beneath her felt strange, neither solid nor soft, as if she were walking on shadows made tangible.

The light grew brighter as she approached, revealing a wide, circular arena carved from black stone. Torches lined the perimeter, their flames flickering with an unnatural, pale blue hue. The air here was heavy with tension, as though the space itself was holding its breath.

At the center of the arena stood Callen. He was alone, his back to her, his head bowed. The glowing markings on his arm pulsed faintly, casting an eerie light across the stone floor. Relief flooded through Evanna at the sight of him.

"Callen!" she called, running toward him.

But before she could reach him, a deafening roar filled the arena, stopping her in her tracks. She froze, her eyes darting around the space as the sound echoed off the walls.

From the shadows, a figure emerged.

—-

The Queen's Champion was unlike anything Evanna had ever seen. Towering and broad-shouldered, it wore blackened armor that seemed to shift and ripple like liquid. The armor was adorned with jagged spikes, and its surface was etched with runes that glowed faintly, pulsing in time with the Champion's movements. Its face was hidden behind a helmet shaped like a snarling beast, and in its hands, it held a massive, double-edged sword that shimmered with an unnatural light.

The Champion moved with a grace that belied its size, stepping into the arena with an air of quiet menace. The ground seemed to tremble beneath its feet, and the very shadows recoiled from its presence.

Evanna's breath caught in her throat. "What is that?" she whispered.

Callen turned to face her, his expression grim. "The Queen's Champion," he said, his voice low and steady. "Her enforcer. Her executioner."

The Champion raised its sword, pointing it directly at Callen. Its voice was deep and guttural, reverberating through the arena like a distant thunderclap. "Wanderer," it growled. "You stand accused of treason against the Queen. Your punishment is death."

—-

Callen stepped forward, his jaw set and his fists clenched. "I won't bow to her," he said, his voice firm. "Not now. Not ever."

The Champion tilted its head, as though considering his words. Then it charged.

The movement was so sudden and forceful that Evanna barely had time to react. The Champion's massive sword swung in a wide arc, its blade cutting through the air with a sharp whistle. Callen dodged just in time, rolling to the side and drawing his own blade in one fluid motion.

The clash of metal rang out as Callen parried the next strike. The force of the impact sent him stumbling backward, but he regained his footing quickly, his movements sharp and precise. Evanna watched in awe as he fought, his every motion filled with a desperation that was both terrifying and inspiring.

But the Champion was relentless. It moved with a speed and precision that seemed impossible for its size, its sword a blur of deadly arcs and thrusts. Each strike pushed Callen closer to the edge of the arena, the glow of his markings intensifying as though feeding off the intensity of the battle.

Evanna's hands trembled as she gripped her dagger, her mind racing. She knew she couldn't just stand there and watch, but the thought of facing the Champion filled her with dread. What could she possibly do against such a foe?

—-

"Evanna!" Callen shouted, his voice breaking through her fear. "The torches—extinguish them!"

She blinked, her gaze snapping to the pale blue flames lining the arena. The torches burned steadily, their light casting long, shifting shadows across the floor.

"Why?" she called back, her voice shaky.

"Just do it!" Callen yelled as he barely dodged another swing of the Champion's blade.

Evanna didn't hesitate. She ran to the nearest torch, her heart pounding as she pulled her cloak around her hand to shield it from the flame. The fire was cold to the touch, and it resisted her efforts, flickering and flaring as though alive. But she persisted, smothering the light until the torch went out.

The effect was immediate. The shadows in the arena shifted, their movements growing more erratic and fragmented. The Champion faltered, its steps unsteady as though it were losing its balance.

Evanna moved quickly to the next torch, repeating the process. One by one, the flames were extinguished, and with each one, the Champion's movements became more sluggish. Its attacks lost their precision, its blade swinging wildly as it struggled to regain control.

By the time the final torch was extinguished, the arena was bathed in near-total darkness. The only light came from the faint glow of Callen's markings and the Champion's runes, which flickered weakly like dying embers.

—-

The Champion roared in frustration, its voice echoing through the darkness. It lunged at Callen, its sword raised for a final strike. But this time, Callen was ready. He sidestepped the attack with a fluid motion, his blade flashing as he struck the Champion's exposed side.

The blow landed with a resounding crack, and the Champion staggered, its armor splintering like glass. Callen pressed the advantage, his movements precise and unrelenting. Each strike chipped away at the Champion's defenses, the glow of his markings growing brighter with every blow.

Evanna watched, her breath caught in her throat as Callen delivered the final strike. His blade pierced through the Champion's chest, and for a moment, time seemed to stand still.

Then, with a deafening roar, the Champion's form shattered into a cloud of shadow and light. The fragments swirled upward, dissolving into the darkness until nothing remained.

—-

The arena fell silent, the oppressive tension lifting like a heavy curtain. Evanna ran to Callen, who was kneeling on the ground, his breathing ragged. His blade slipped from his hand, clattering against the stone floor.

"Are you okay?" she asked, her voice thick with concern.

Callen looked up at her, his expression weary but triumphant. "I'm alive," he said, a faint smile tugging at the corners of his mouth. "That's enough for now."

Evanna helped him to his feet, her hands shaking as the adrenaline coursing through her veins began to fade. Together, they stood in the center of the arena, the darkness around them seeming less oppressive now.

"We need to keep moving," Callen said, his voice steady despite his exhaustion. "The Queen will know we're here."

Evanna nodded, her resolve hardening. The fight with the Champion had shown her just how dangerous the Court of Endless Dusk could be. But it had also shown her something else: that they were capable of defying it.

As they left the arena, the faint echo of the Champion's roar lingered in the air, a haunting reminder of the battle they had just survived—and the trials that still lay ahead.

Eight

The Shattered Memory

The path beyond the arena was a narrow corridor carved from black stone, its walls etched with glowing runes that pulsed faintly in the oppressive darkness. Evanna and Callen walked in silence, their footsteps echoing softly in the still air. The weight of the battle with the Queen's Champion hung heavy between them, and neither dared to speak. The Vale seemed to hum with an unseen energy, as though it were alive and aware of their presence.

Callen's movements were slow and deliberate, his hand occasionally brushing against the glowing markings on his arm. The battle had taken its toll on him, though he refused to show it. His jaw was set, his eyes focused on the path ahead, but Evanna could see the tension in his posture, the weariness that threatened to overtake him.

"You need to rest," she said, her voice gentle but firm.

"I can't," Callen replied without looking at her. "Not here. Not yet."

Evanna frowned but didn't argue. The Vale was no place for vulnerability, and she knew Callen well enough by now to understand that he wouldn't stop unless he had no other choice. Instead, she walked beside him, her dagger gripped tightly in her hand, ready for whatever might come next.

—-

They emerged from the corridor into a wide, open chamber bathed in an eerie, shifting light. The floor was covered in shallow pools of water, their surfaces perfectly still and reflective like mirrors. The air here was colder, and a faint mist clung to the ground, swirling around their feet as they moved.

"This place..." Callen murmured, his voice trailing off as he looked around.

"What is it?" Evanna asked, her eyes scanning the chamber for any signs of danger.

Callen hesitated, his gaze fixed on the pools. "It's a memory chamber," he said finally. "A place where the Court keeps fragments of the past. Moments torn from time."

Evanna's breath caught, her grip on her dagger tightening.

"Whose memories?"

"Anyone who's crossed the Queen," Callen said, his voice low. "Anyone she wanted to control."

Evanna shivered, her mind racing with the implications. The chamber felt alive, the pools of water pulsing faintly as though in rhythm with her heartbeat. She stepped cautiously toward one of the pools, her reflection rippling slightly as she approached.

"Don't touch it," Callen warned, his voice sharp.

Evanna stopped, her eyes flickering to his. "Why not?"

"The memories aren't just images," he said. "They pull you in. If you're not careful, you'll get lost in them."

Evanna nodded, though her curiosity burned. The pools seemed to whisper to her, their surfaces shimmering with hints of movement, flashes of color and light that were almost too quick to catch. She forced herself to look away, focusing instead on Callen, who stood at the edge of another pool, his expression unreadable.

"Callen…" she began, but her words were cut off as the surface of the pool nearest him began to glow.

—-

The light from the pool intensified, spreading outward in

rippling waves. Evanna took a step back, her heart pounding as the air around them seemed to shift. The chamber grew darker, the light from the pool casting long, flickering shadows across the walls.

"What's happening?" she demanded, her voice rising.

Callen didn't answer. His gaze was fixed on the pool, his body rigid as though frozen in place. The light coalesced into a vivid image, a memory that played out before them like a scene from a dream.

The throne room appeared first, grand and imposing, its walls lined with dark banners bearing the sigil of the Queen. At the center of the room sat the Queen herself, her golden eyes gleaming with a cold, predatory light. She was speaking to someone—a man who knelt before her, his head bowed.

Evanna's breath caught as she recognized the man. It was Callen.

"This isn't real," Evanna said, her voice trembling. "It's just a memory."

But Callen didn't respond. His hands were clenched into fists, his breathing shallow and uneven. Evanna took a step toward him, but before she could reach him, the scene in the pool shifted.

The kneeling Callen looked up at the Queen, his expression a mixture of fear and defiance. "I won't do it," he said, his voice shaking. "You can't make me."

The Queen smiled, a slow, cruel curve of her lips. "Oh, my dear Callen," she purred. "You overestimate your will. You will serve me, whether you wish to or not."

The memory blurred, and the scene changed. Callen was standing in a grand hall, surrounded by shadowy figures. He held a blade in his hand, its edge stained with blood. His eyes were wide with horror as he stared down at the bodies on the floor—men and women who had once stood with him.

"No…" Callen whispered, his voice barely audible. "No, I didn't…"

Evanna felt a chill run through her as the memory played out. The shadowy figures in the memory began to turn toward Callen, their faces obscured but their voices clear.

"Why did you betray us?" one voice hissed.

"You were supposed to protect us," another said, filled with venom.

Callen stumbled back, his hands clutching his head as though trying to block out the voices. "It wasn't me," he said, his voice breaking. "It wasn't me!"

—-

Evanna rushed to his side, grabbing his arm and pulling him

away from the pool. "Callen, look at me!" she said, her voice firm. "It's not real. It's just a memory. Whatever happened, it's in the past."

Callen's eyes met hers, filled with anguish and guilt. "I don't remember," he said, his voice trembling. "I don't remember if it's true."

"It doesn't matter," Evanna said, her grip on his arm tightening. "You're here now. Whatever the Queen did to you, whatever she made you do, you're not her pawn anymore."

Callen nodded slowly, his breathing evening out. The light from the pool faded, and the chamber returned to its dim, mist-filled state.

—-

As they moved away from the pools, Evanna couldn't shake the feeling that the chamber had taken something from them—something intangible but vital. The air felt heavier, the whispers in the distance more insistent.

"Why would the Queen keep these memories here?" Evanna asked, breaking the silence.

"To control us," Callen said, his voice quiet but steady. "The memories keep you tied to her. They make you doubt yourself, your choices. It's how she keeps her hold."

Evanna glanced at him, her heart aching at the pain in his eyes.

"We'll find a way to break her hold," she said. "Whatever it takes."

Callen didn't respond, but the faint flicker of hope in his expression was enough to keep her going.

—-

As they left the chamber, the path ahead seemed darker, more foreboding. The Vale felt alive, its shadows pressing closer, its whispers louder. But Evanna and Callen walked on, their resolve unshaken.

The Queen's power was vast, her reach long, but they were determined to face her. Together.

Nine

A Deal with Shadows

The atmosphere in the Vale grew heavier as Evanna and Callen trudged forward, the oppressive shadows pressing closer with every step. The path had narrowed to a twisting corridor lined with jagged, crystalline formations that glimmered faintly with a pale, otherworldly light. Each step seemed to echo endlessly, as if the Vale itself were mocking their progress.

Evanna's mind raced as she tried to make sense of everything they had encountered—the Court's trials, the Champion, the shattered memories. Each moment felt like it had been designed to break them, to pull them apart, and she couldn't shake the feeling that they were walking into a trap.

Beside her, Callen remained silent, his gaze fixed on the path ahead. His face was pale, and the glow of the markings on his arm had dimmed, as though even they were losing strength. He had spoken little since the memory chamber, and though Evanna wanted to press him, she knew better than to push.

"We're getting close," Callen said suddenly, his voice low and strained.

Evanna glanced at him. "Close to what?"

"The Queen," he replied. "Or one of her emissaries. This part of the Vale feels… tainted. It's where her influence is strongest."

Evanna shivered, pulling her cloak tighter around her shoulders. The Vale seemed alive here, the shadows shifting and writhing as if they were watching them, waiting for the perfect moment to strike.

—-

They came to a sudden stop at the edge of a massive clearing. In the center stood a circular platform made of dark stone, its surface etched with runes that pulsed with a faint crimson glow. Surrounding the platform were tall, twisted pillars that seemed to radiate an unnatural cold, their tops vanishing into the swirling mists above.

At the far end of the clearing, a figure emerged from the shadows.

It was a woman—or at least, she had the shape of one. Her form was shrouded in a flowing black gown that seemed to merge with the darkness around her. Her face was partially obscured by a veil of shadows, but her eyes burned like molten gold, piercing and unrelenting. She moved with an unnatural grace, her steps silent despite the weight of her presence.

"Callen," the figure said, her voice smooth and melodic, yet laced with an undercurrent of menace. "You've returned to us at last."

Callen stiffened, his hand instinctively moving to the hilt of his blade. "I didn't come back for you, Nyssara," he said coldly. "And I'm not here to bargain."

Nyssara tilted her head, her eyes gleaming with amusement. "No? And yet, here you are, walking willingly into the shadow of the Court. How curious."

Evanna stepped forward, her dagger clutched tightly in her hand. "Who are you?" she demanded, her voice steady despite the fear coiling in her chest.

Nyssara turned her gaze to Evanna, her smile widening. "I am Nyssara, the Keeper of Promises. A servant of the Queen, though some would call me her shadow." She looked Evanna up and down, her expression unreadable. "And you must be the healer. An odd companion for a traitor."

Evanna's grip on her dagger tightened, but she held her ground. "We're not here to play games," she said. "If you have something to say, say it."

Nyssara's smile faded, and her golden eyes narrowed. "Very well," she said, her tone icy. "You have trespassed deep into the Vale, defied the Queen's trials, and slain her Champion. Such defiance cannot go unanswered."

"We're not afraid of her," Callen said, his voice sharp.

Nyssara laughed, a soft, melodic sound that sent a chill down Evanna's spine. "Oh, my dear Callen, your fear is not what I seek. It is your submission."

—-

Nyssara raised her hand, and the air around them seemed to ripple. The runes on the platform flared brightly, and from the shadows emerged a figure—a spectral form, translucent and wreathed in faint, silvery light. Evanna's breath caught as she recognized the face.

"Mother?"

The figure's expression was blank, its eyes unseeing, but its presence was unmistakable. Evanna took a step forward, her heart pounding.

"It can't be," she whispered.

Nyssara's voice cut through the air like a blade. "The Vale holds many secrets, healer. Memories, fragments, echoes of the past. Your mother's essence lingers here, tied to the choices you made... or failed to make."

Evanna turned to Nyssara, her eyes blazing with anger. "What do you want?"

Nyssara smiled, her gaze shifting between Evanna and Callen. "A deal," she said simply. "The Queen is merciful, even to those who defy her. She offers you a choice: return what was stolen, and you may leave this place unscathed."

"And what exactly was stolen?" Callen demanded.

Nyssara's smile widened. "You, of course," she said. "The Queen's favored creation. Her loyal enforcer. You belong to her, Callen, and it's time you returned to your place."

Callen's jaw tightened, his hand gripping the hilt of his blade. "I'd rather die."

Nyssara's expression darkened, her eyes glowing brighter. "That can be arranged."

—-

The air grew colder, and the shadows around the platform began to coalesce, forming into humanoid shapes. They moved with an eerie grace, their features indistinct but their intent clear.

Evanna stepped closer to Callen, her dagger raised. "What do we do?" she asked, her voice trembling.

Callen's gaze remained fixed on Nyssara. "We fight," he said.

Nyssara laughed again, the sound echoing through the clearing. "You cannot fight shadows, Callen," she said. "But if you insist on defiance, then so be it."

She raised her hand, and the shadowy figures surged forward.

—-

The battle was chaos. The shadows moved with unnatural speed, their forms shifting and twisting as they attacked. Evanna fought desperately, her dagger slicing through the air as she tried to fend them off. Each strike disrupted the shadows, but they re-formed just as quickly, their attacks relentless.

Callen moved with a precision born of desperation, his blade flashing as he fought off the shadowy attackers. The glow of the markings on his arm intensified, and with each strike, the shadows seemed to recoil slightly, as though his power was repelling them.

"Evanna!" he shouted, his voice cutting through the din. "Get to the platform!"

Evanna hesitated, her eyes darting to the glowing runes. The platform pulsed with energy, its light flickering in time with the movements of the shadows.

"What do I do?" she called back.

"Trust me!" Callen shouted.

—-

Evanna ran to the platform, dodging the shadows as they lunged at her. She climbed onto the stone, her heart racing as the energy from the runes surged through her. The light grew brighter, and the shadows faltered, their forms wavering.

Nyssara's voice rang out, sharp and furious. "You dare defy the Queen's will?"

Evanna didn't respond. She knelt by the runes, her hands trembling as she traced the glowing symbols. Instinctively, she began to speak words she didn't understand, her voice steady despite the chaos around her.

The runes flared brightly, and the shadows dissolved, their forms dissipating into the air. Nyssara let out a furious scream, her form flickering as though she were losing her connection to the Vale.

"This is not over," Nyssara hissed, her golden eyes blazing with fury. "The Queen will not be denied."

With a final, piercing glare, Nyssara vanished, leaving the clearing in silence.

—-

Evanna collapsed onto the platform, her body trembling with exhaustion. Callen joined her moments later, his blade slick with dark, shadowy ichor.

"Are you okay?" he asked, his voice rough.

Evanna nodded, though her hands still shook. "What was that?"

Callen sighed, his gaze distant. "A taste of what's to come."

Evanna shivered, her mind racing. They had survived Nyssara's trial, but the Queen's shadow still loomed over them.

The Vale was not done with them yet.

Ten

The Maze of Fates

The clearing was eerily silent after Nyssara's departure, the oppressive weight of her presence lingering like a phantom. The runes on the stone platform still pulsed faintly, their light dimming as the shadows dissipated into the Vale. Evanna and Callen sat in the aftermath of the confrontation, their breaths coming in ragged gasps. The ordeal had left them shaken but resolute.

"We need to keep moving," Callen said after a moment, his voice hoarse but determined.

Evanna nodded, wiping sweat from her brow as she stood. "Where to?"

Callen gestured toward the path that led beyond the platform, a narrow, twisting trail that seemed to disappear into the shadows. "The Maze of Fates," he said grimly. "It's the only way forward."

Evanna's stomach turned at the name. "Maze of Fates? That doesn't sound promising."

"It's not," Callen admitted, his expression dark. "But it's the last trial before the heart of the Court. If we make it through, we'll be within reach of the Queen's domain."

The weight of his words settled over them as they stepped off the platform and into the waiting shadows.

—-

The entrance to the maze was marked by a towering archway made of jagged, black stone. Strange carvings covered its surface—faces frozen in expressions of terror and anguish, their features grotesque and distorted. Evanna hesitated at the threshold, a chill running down her spine as she stared at the archway.

"What is this place?" she asked, her voice barely above a whisper.

"The Maze of Fates," Callen repeated. "It's a construct of the Court. A living maze that tests those who dare to challenge the Queen. It reacts to your thoughts, your fears... your weaknesses."

Evanna frowned, gripping the hilt of her dagger tightly. "And how do we get through it?"

Callen's gaze was steady but uncertain. "We don't. The maze decides if we're worthy of passage."

The words sent a shiver through Evanna. She glanced at the maze, its shadowy corridors twisting and shifting as though alive. There was no telling what waited for them inside—or if they would ever find their way out.

—-

The moment they stepped through the archway, the air changed. The oppressive cold of the Vale deepened, seeping into their bones, and the faint whispers that had accompanied them since entering the Court became louder, more distinct. The ground beneath their feet was uneven, a patchwork of stone and shifting sand that seemed to shift with each step.

The maze stretched out before them, its corridors narrow and winding. High walls of black stone towered on either side, their surfaces slick and gleaming as though coated in oil. Strange, flickering lights danced along the edges of the path, casting long, shifting shadows that seemed to move of their own accord.

"This place..." Evanna began, her voice trailing off as she struggled to find the words.

"Don't trust anything you see or hear," Callen said, his tone sharp. "The maze is designed to confuse you, to play tricks on your mind. Stay close to me, and don't look back."

Evanna nodded, her grip on her dagger tightening as they began their journey through the maze.

—-

At first, the path seemed straightforward, the corridors twisting and turning but ultimately leading forward. But as they ventured deeper, the maze began to change. The walls seemed to shift and breathe, closing in around them and then expanding without warning. The floor beneath their feet rippled like water, making every step feel precarious.

The whispers grew louder, their tones taking on an almost human quality. Evanna could make out words now, fragmented sentences that seemed to come from all directions.

"Why didn't you save me?" one voice hissed, low and venomous.

"You don't belong here," another whispered, soft and mocking.

Evanna clenched her fists, forcing herself to ignore the voices. But with each step, they grew more insistent, their words cutting deeper into her mind.

—-

The first true challenge came when the path split into three. Each corridor was identical, their darkened passages stretching out into the unknown. Callen stopped, his eyes scanning the paths as though searching for a clue.

"Which way?" Evanna asked, her voice trembling.

Callen hesitated, his gaze flickering to the markings on his arm. They glowed faintly, their light pulsing in rhythm with the whispers that surrounded them. "I don't know," he admitted. "The maze doesn't give you directions. It's meant to test your instincts."

Evanna frowned, her heart pounding as she looked at the three paths. "What happens if we choose wrong?"

"We don't get another chance," Callen said grimly.

The weight of his words hung between them as they stood at the crossroads, the maze seeming to watch their every move. Finally, Callen stepped forward, his gaze fixed on the middle path. "This way," he said, his voice steady.

Evanna followed without hesitation, her trust in Callen outweighing her fear.

—-

The path grew narrower as they ventured deeper, the walls closing in until they were forced to walk single file. The air grew colder, and the whispers gave way to a low, droning hum that seemed to vibrate through the very stone.

"Do you hear that?" Evanna asked, her voice barely audible.

Callen nodded, his hand resting on the hilt of his blade. "It's the maze. It's testing us."

Before Evanna could respond, the path opened into a circular chamber. At its center stood a pedestal, and atop it rested a small, black orb that pulsed with a faint, crimson light. The walls of the chamber were lined with mirrors, their surfaces reflecting not the room but distorted, nightmarish versions of themselves.

Evanna froze, her breath catching in her throat as she stared at the mirrors. In each reflection, she saw herself twisted and broken—her face lined with anguish, her hands stained with blood.

"Don't look at them," Callen warned, his voice sharp. "They're not real."

Evanna tore her gaze away, her hands trembling as she focused on the orb. "What is that?" she asked, her voice shaking.

"A choice," Callen said. "The maze always offers a choice."

As if on cue, a voice echoed through the chamber, deep and resonant. "Take the orb, and your passage will be granted. Refuse, and the shadows will claim you."

Evanna glanced at Callen, her mind racing. "What do we do?"

Callen's gaze was fixed on the orb, his expression unreadable. "If we take it, we bind ourselves to the maze. It might let us pass, but it'll mark us. The Queen will know exactly where we are."

"And if we don't?"

Callen's jaw tightened. "Then we find another way."

Evanna hesitated, her heart pounding as the voice echoed again. "Choose quickly, or the maze will choose for you."

—-

Before she could think, the shadows in the chamber began to shift, coalescing into humanoid forms that moved with an eerie grace. Their eyes burned with a cold, pale light, and their movements were unnervingly synchronized.

"Evanna," Callen said, his voice urgent. "We have to move."

"But the orb—"

"Forget the orb!" Callen shouted, grabbing her arm and pulling her toward one of the mirrored walls. To Evanna's shock, the surface of the mirror rippled like water as Callen pressed his hand against it. "This way!" he said, stepping through.

Evanna hesitated for only a moment before following him, the mirror's surface enveloping her like a cold, viscous liquid.

—-

They emerged in another corridor, the whispers returning with a vengeance. The shadows behind them clawed at the edges of the mirror, but they didn't follow. Evanna stumbled, her heart racing as Callen steadied her.

"What just happened?" she demanded, her voice shaking.

"The maze doesn't just test you," Callen said, his tone grim. "It tries to trap you. The orb was a distraction—a way to keep us here forever."

Evanna shivered, her mind reeling as they continued down the path. The maze had shown its true nature, and she knew now that it wouldn't let them leave easily.

As they pressed on, the shadows seemed to close in, the whispers growing louder, more insistent. The maze was alive, and it wasn't done with them yet.

Eleven

Secrets Beneath the Veil

The corridor beyond the mirrored wall stretched endlessly, a narrow path carved through the shadows. The whispers had dulled to a faint murmur, but they still lingered at the edges of Evanna's mind, unsettling in their persistence. The air was colder now, sharp and biting against her skin, as though the maze itself was warning her that they had strayed into forbidden territory.

Callen walked ahead, his movements cautious and deliberate. The faint glow of the markings on his arm illuminated the path in pale, shifting light, casting long shadows on the walls. Evanna followed closely, her dagger clutched tightly in her hand, her heart pounding with each step.

"What was that thing in the chamber?" she asked after a long silence, her voice barely above a whisper.

"The orb?" Callen glanced back at her, his expression grim. "It was a lure. The maze uses objects like that to test your will—or trap you. If we'd taken it, we'd have been bound to this place forever."

Evanna shivered, her fingers tightening around the hilt of her dagger. "It felt… wrong. Like it was alive."

Callen nodded. "That's because it was. Everything in the maze is connected to the Queen's power. It's all a part of her design."

They continued in silence, the oppressive atmosphere of the maze pressing down on them like a physical weight. The walls seemed to pulse faintly, their surfaces slick and dark, as though they were breathing. Evanna tried to ignore the sensation, but it was impossible to shake the feeling that they were being watched.

—-

The path eventually opened into a vast, cavernous chamber, its ceiling lost in the swirling mists above. The floor was uneven, a patchwork of jagged stone and shallow pools of water that reflected the faint, flickering light of the room's many torches. At the center of the chamber stood a massive, intricately carved pedestal, its surface covered in glowing runes.

Evanna and Callen approached the pedestal cautiously, their eyes scanning the room for any signs of danger. The air here was thick with tension, and the faint hum of energy vibrated through the stone beneath their feet.

"What is this place?" Evanna asked, her voice trembling.

Callen hesitated, his gaze fixed on the pedestal. "A repository," he said finally. "A place where the Queen stores secrets—fragments of knowledge she doesn't want anyone to find."

Evanna's stomach turned at the thought. "Why would she keep them here? In the maze?"

"Because no one who enters the maze is supposed to leave," Callen said darkly.

—-

As they neared the pedestal, the runes began to glow brighter, their light casting strange, shifting patterns across the chamber walls. Evanna felt a strange pull, an almost magnetic force drawing her toward the pedestal. Her steps faltered, her heart pounding as she fought the urge to move closer.

"Careful," Callen warned, his hand on the hilt of his blade. "The pedestal isn't just a repository. It's a trap."

Evanna frowned, her eyes flickering to the runes. "A trap for what?"

"For the truth," Callen said, his voice low. "The Queen uses places like this to hide the things she doesn't want anyone to know. But if you get too close, the pedestal shows you things—secrets, memories, visions. And once you've seen them, you can't unsee them."

Evanna hesitated, the pull of the pedestal growing stronger. "What kind of secrets?"

Callen's expression darkened. "The kind that change every-thing."

—-

Despite his warning, Evanna stepped closer to the pedestal, her curiosity outweighing her fear. The runes flared brighter as she approached, their light pulsating in time with her heartbeat. She reached out, her fingers brushing against the cool, smooth surface.

The moment her skin made contact, the chamber was filled with a blinding light. Evanna stumbled back, her vision swim-ming as images flooded her mind—fragments of memories, half-formed thoughts, and cryptic symbols that seemed to burn into her consciousness.

She saw the Queen, her golden eyes cold and unyielding, standing in a grand hall surrounded by shadowy figures. She saw Callen kneeling before her, his face twisted with anguish as he spoke words she couldn't hear. She saw herself, standing in the Vale, her hands stained with blood as the shadows closed in around her.

And then, she saw something else—something that made her blood run cold. A figure stood in the heart of the Court, cloaked in darkness, its face obscured but its presence unmistakably powerful. The figure raised a hand, and the entire Vale seemed to shudder, the shadows recoiling as though in fear.

Evanna gasped, her knees buckling as the vision faded. She felt Callen's hands on her shoulders, steadying her as she struggled to catch her breath.

"What did you see?" he asked, his voice urgent.

Evanna shook her head, her mind reeling. "I don't know," she said, her voice trembling. "It was… pieces of something. The Queen. You. And someone else."

"Someone else?" Callen's brow furrowed. "Who?"

"I don't know," Evanna said again, her hands trembling. "But they were powerful. Like they controlled the shadows."

Callen's expression darkened, his gaze flickering to the pedestal. "The pedestal doesn't show you random visions," he said. "It shows you the truth. If you saw someone in the Court, it means they're important."

Evanna's stomach churned at the thought. "Important to what?"

"To the Queen," Callen said grimly. "And to us."

—-

Before Evanna could respond, the ground beneath their feet began to shake. The runes on the pedestal flared brighter, and the air was filled with a low, resonant hum that grew louder with each passing second.

"We need to move," Callen said, his voice urgent. "The pedestal's activating."

Evanna didn't need to be told twice. She turned and ran, following Callen as he led them away from the chamber and back into the twisting corridors of the maze. The hum grew louder behind them, the walls vibrating as though the maze itself was coming alive.

The shadows pressed closer as they ran, their movements frantic and chaotic. Evanna could hear the whispers growing louder, their tones sharp and angry. She gritted her teeth, forcing herself to focus on Callen and the path ahead.

—-

They emerged into another chamber, smaller and darker than the first. The walls here were covered in strange, glowing symbols that seemed to writhe and shift like living things. At the center of the room stood a tall, narrow mirror, its surface perfectly smooth and reflective.

Callen froze, his eyes narrowing as he stared at the mirror. "This isn't right," he muttered. "The maze is changing."

"What do you mean?" Evanna asked, her voice shaking.

Callen didn't answer. Instead, he stepped closer to the mirror, his reflection rippling as though the surface were made of water.

He reached out, his hand hovering just above the glass.

"Callen, don't—" Evanna began, but it was too late.

The moment his fingers touched the mirror, the room was filled with a blinding light. Evanna shielded her eyes, her heart pounding as the light faded to reveal a new scene.

They were no longer in the maze. They stood in a grand hall, its walls lined with dark banners bearing the sigil of the Queen. At the far end of the hall was a throne, and seated upon it was the Queen herself, her golden eyes glowing with malice.

"Welcome," she said, her voice smooth and cold. "I've been expecting you."

Evanna and Callen exchanged a glance, their blood running cold.

The maze had delivered them directly into the heart of the Court.

Twelve

The Queen's Masquerade

T he grand hall of the Queen's Court loomed before Evanna and Callen, a space so vast it seemed to stretch into eternity. Massive columns of black stone lined the room, their surfaces carved with intricate runes that pulsed faintly with a golden glow. The walls were adorned with banners bearing the sigil of the Queen—a crown encircled by shadowy tendrils—and the air was heavy with the scent of incense, sharp and intoxicating.

At the far end of the hall stood a throne of twisted obsidian, its jagged edges gleaming in the dim light. Seated upon it was the Queen herself, her presence commanding and terrifying. Her golden eyes burned with an unnatural intensity, and her gown of flowing black silk seemed to merge with the shadows around her, as though she were part of the Court itself.

Evanna felt her breath catch as the Queen's gaze fell upon her. There was something deeply unsettling about those eyes—something that saw through her, stripping away her defenses and laying her soul bare.

"Welcome," the Queen said, her voice smooth and melodic, yet laced with an undercurrent of menace. "You've traveled far to reach me. Few make it this far."

Callen stepped forward, his jaw set and his fists clenched. "We're not here to play your games," he said, his voice steady despite the tension in his posture.

The Queen tilted her head, a faint smile playing at her lips. "Oh, but you've already played, haven't you? The trials, the maze, the memories—those were my games, and you chose to participate."

Evanna glanced at Callen, her stomach churning with unease. The Queen's words carried a weight that was impossible to ignore, and the realization that they had been walking into her trap all along sent a chill down her spine.

—-

Before either of them could respond, the Queen clapped her hands, the sharp sound echoing through the hall. At once, the shadows around them shifted, forming into humanoid shapes that began to move with an eerie grace. Music filled the air, a haunting melody played on unseen instruments, and the figures took their places, circling Evanna and Callen like dancers at a masquerade.

The figures wore masks of polished gold, each one intricately designed and unique. Their movements were fluid and hypnotic, their silent presence amplifying the tension in the room.

"A masquerade," the Queen said, rising from her throne with an elegant sweep of her gown. "A celebration in honor of your arrival. After all, it's not every day that mortals dare to defy me."

Evanna's grip tightened on her dagger as she watched the dancers. Their movements were too precise, too perfect, as though they were being controlled by invisible strings. She felt a strange pull, an almost magnetic force that made it difficult to look away.

"What do you want from us?" she asked, her voice steady despite the fear coursing through her veins.

The Queen descended the steps of her throne, her golden eyes locked onto Evanna. "What I want," she said, her voice as smooth as silk, "is already mine. You are here because I allowed it. You are alive because I willed it. And now, you will play your part."

Evanna's heart pounded as the Queen stopped in front of her, towering over her like a shadow made flesh. The dancers continued to circle them, their golden masks gleaming in the flickering light.

"What part?" Callen demanded, stepping protectively between Evanna and the Queen.

The Queen's smile widened, her gaze shifting to Callen. "Ah, my dear Callen. Always so defiant, so determined to fight the inevitable. You were mine once, and you will be again."

Callen's jaw tightened, his hand resting on the hilt of his blade. "Never."

The Queen chuckled, a low, melodic sound that sent shivers down Evanna's spine. "We shall see."

—-

The Queen clapped her hands again, and the music shifted, its tempo quickening. The dancers moved closer, their golden masks reflecting the dim light as they closed in around Evanna and Callen.

"The rules are simple," the Queen said, her voice carrying over the music. "The masquerade is a game of truth and deception. You will dance, and as you do, the masks will reveal your secrets. If you survive until the final note, you may leave. If not…" Her smile turned sharp, her golden eyes gleaming with malice. "The shadows will claim you."

Evanna's breath caught. "And if we refuse?"

The Queen raised a hand, and the shadows around the room surged forward, coiling like living snakes. "Refusal is not an option."

Callen drew his blade, the glowing markings on his arm flaring brightly. "We'll fight if we have to."

The Queen's laugh was sharp and cold. "Oh, Callen. The Court does not fight. It consumes."

—-

Before either of them could react, the shadows enveloped them, pulling them apart. Evanna struggled against the cold, suffocating darkness, her dagger useless against the intangible force. When the shadows receded, she found herself standing in the center of the hall, surrounded by the masked dancers.

Her dagger was gone, and her hands trembled as she looked around. Callen was nowhere in sight, and the realization sent a fresh wave of panic through her.

"Let the masquerade begin," the Queen's voice echoed, and the music swelled.

One of the masked dancers stepped forward, extending a hand to Evanna. She hesitated, her heart pounding, but the pull of the game was irresistible. Reluctantly, she took the dancer's hand, and the dance began.

—-

The dancer moved with a fluid grace, leading Evanna in a series of intricate steps. The golden mask hid its features, but its presence was overpowering, its movements guiding her as though she were a puppet on a string.

As they danced, the mask began to change. Its surface rippled like liquid gold, and images appeared—fragments of memories that made Evanna's blood run cold.

She saw herself as a child, standing at the edge of the Vale, her mother's voice calling her back. She saw the moment her mother fell ill, the fear and helplessness that had consumed her. And then she saw the day her mother died, her hand clutching Evanna's as she drew her final breath.

"You could have saved her," a voice whispered, low and accusatory.

Evanna stumbled, her breath catching as the memory played out before her. "No," she said, her voice trembling. "I tried. I did everything I could."

The mask shifted, its golden surface reflecting her anguished expression. "Did you? Or were you too afraid?"

—-

The music quickened, and the dance became more frantic. The other dancers closed in, their masks glowing as they whispered fragments of her past, her fears, her failures.

"You left her to die."

"You weren't strong enough."

"She suffered because of you."

Evanna's vision blurred, tears streaming down her face as the weight of their words pressed down on her. She tried to pull away, but the dancer's grip was unyielding.

And then, just as the music reached its peak, the mask cracked.

The golden surface shattered, revealing a face beneath—a face that was her own, twisted and broken. Evanna gasped, her heart pounding as she stared at her doppelgänger.

"You are your own worst enemy," the reflection said, its voice cold and hollow.

—-

The music stopped abruptly, and the dancers froze. The room was silent, save for the sound of Evanna's ragged breathing.

The Queen's laughter echoed through the hall, sharp and mocking. "Well done, healer," she said, stepping forward. "You've survived the first round. But there is more yet to come."

Evanna sank to her knees, her body trembling as the weight of the game settled over her. The masquerade was far from over, and the shadows of the Court were closing in.

And somewhere in the darkness, Callen was fighting his own battle.

Thirteen

Dance of Betrayal

The haunting melody resumed, filling the grand hall with an otherworldly resonance that seemed to seep into Evanna's very bones. The golden masks of the dancers shimmered with a spectral light as they began to move again, their steps slow and deliberate. The Queen remained at the edge of the dance floor, her golden eyes gleaming with a dangerous mix of amusement and malice.

Evanna staggered to her feet, her heart racing as the masked figures swayed around her in a hypnotic rhythm. The memory of her doppelgänger's haunting words still clung to her like a shadow, but she forced herself to focus. She couldn't afford to fall apart—not now.

"Where's Callen?" she demanded, her voice trembling but resolute.

The Queen smiled, her gaze as sharp as a blade. "He is dancing his own dance, healer. Just as you are."

The cryptic answer sent a chill down Evanna's spine. She turned, her eyes scanning the shifting crowd of dancers, hoping to catch a glimpse of him. But the figures around her moved like liquid shadows, their forms blending seamlessly with the flickering light of the hall. It was impossible to tell where one ended and another began.

"Let him go," Evanna said, her voice rising. "This is between you and me."

The Queen's laughter rang out, cold and mocking. "Oh, my dear, you misunderstand. This is not a game you play alone. The Court is a stage, and all who enter it must perform. Your partner is here, but whether he stands with you or against you… that is yet to be seen."

—-

Before Evanna could respond, one of the masked dancers stepped forward, extending a hand to her. The figure's movements were elegant, almost seductive, and the golden mask reflected her own face, distorted and fractured.

"You must dance," the Queen said, her voice commanding. "The truth lies within the steps. The betrayal lies within the music."

Evanna hesitated, her instincts screaming at her to run. But there was no escape—the shadows pressed in from all sides, and the air itself seemed to thrum with the Queen's power.

Reluctantly, she took the dancer's hand.

—-

The moment their hands touched, the world shifted.

The grand hall dissolved into a swirling void of light and shadow, and Evanna found herself standing on a narrow, circular platform suspended in endless darkness. The masked dancer stood across from her, its golden face gleaming in the faint light.

"Where are we?" Evanna asked, her voice echoing unnaturally.

The dancer said nothing. Instead, it began to move, its steps slow and deliberate, its body swaying to a rhythm that seemed to come from the void itself. The music was different here— sharper, more discordant, like the sound of glass shattering in slow motion.

Evanna hesitated, unsure of what to do. But then the dancer lunged, its movements suddenly sharp and aggressive. She stumbled back, barely avoiding its grasp, and realized with a jolt that this was not a simple dance.

This was a battle.

—-

The dancer moved with inhuman speed, its golden mask glowing brighter with each step. Evanna ducked and weaved, her heart pounding as she tried to keep up. Her dagger was gone, leaving her defenseless against the figure's relentless attacks.

"What do you want?" she shouted, her voice filled with desperation.

The dancer didn't answer. Instead, it struck again, its movements fluid and precise. Evanna managed to dodge, but the edge of the platform crumbled beneath her foot, and she barely regained her balance.

"You must dance," a voice whispered, low and insistent. "The truth lies within the steps."

Evanna gritted her teeth, forcing herself to move. She mimicked the dancer's steps, her body following the erratic rhythm of the music. At first, it felt awkward and unnatural, but as she continued, she began to notice a pattern—an underlying harmony hidden within the chaos.

The dancer's movements slowed, its attacks becoming less forceful. The light of its mask flickered, and for a moment, Evanna thought she saw something beneath the golden surface—a pair of piercing blue eyes.

"Callen?" she whispered, her voice barely audible.

The dancer froze, its body trembling. The mask rippled like

liquid gold, and the figure stepped back, its hands reaching for its face. Slowly, it removed the mask, revealing Callen's face beneath. His expression was a mixture of anguish and relief, his eyes filled with pain.

"It's me," he said, his voice breaking. "Evanna, it's me."

—-

Evanna's breath caught as she stared at him. "What's going on? Why are you—" She stopped, her mind racing. The Queen's words echoed in her ears: Your partner is here, but whether he stands with you or against you… that is yet to be seen.

"She made me do it," Callen said, his voice trembling. "The Queen… she controls this place. She made me fight you."

Evanna took a cautious step forward, her heart aching at the sight of him. "It's okay," she said gently. "I'm here. We'll get through this together."

Callen shook his head, his expression darkening. "You don't understand. She made me see things—things I didn't want to remember. And now… she's in my head. I can't stop her."

Evanna's stomach turned. "What do you mean?"

Before Callen could answer, the void around them shuddered, and the Queen's laughter filled the air. "Ah, how touching," she said, her voice dripping with mockery. "But the dance is not yet finished."

The platform beneath them began to crack, fissures spreading across its surface as the music grew louder and more chaotic. The shadows around them surged, coiling like living snakes.

"Evanna, listen to me," Callen said urgently. "Whatever happens, you can't trust me. The Queen's hold on me—it's stronger than I thought."

Evanna's heart clenched, but she nodded. "I trust you," she said. "Even if you don't trust yourself."

The platform shattered, and they plunged into darkness.

—-

Evanna awoke on the cold stone floor of the grand hall, the sound of the haunting melody still ringing in her ears. The dancers were gone, their golden masks scattered across the floor like fallen leaves. The Queen stood at the edge of the room, her golden eyes gleaming with triumph.

"Well played," she said, her voice smooth and taunting. "But the game is far from over."

Evanna pushed herself to her feet, her body trembling. She glanced around, her heart sinking when she realized Callen was nowhere to be seen.

"Where is he?" she demanded, her voice shaking with fury.

The Queen smiled, a cold and cruel expression. "He is where

he belongs—on the edge of betrayal, teetering between loyalty and defiance. A perfect pawn in my game."

Evanna's fists clenched, her anger boiling over. "This isn't a game to us."

"Everything is a game," the Queen said, her tone sharp. "And the Court always wins."

Evanna's resolve hardened as she stared at the Queen. She didn't know how, but she would find Callen, and she would end this. The Queen's reign of shadows would not go unchallenged.

The dance of betrayal had begun, but the final steps were yet to be written.

Fourteen

The Keeper of Truths

The silence in the wake of the Queen's laughter was deafening. Evanna stood in the center of the grand hall, her chest heaving with exhaustion and anger. The scattered masks of the dancers gleamed faintly in the dim light, each one a silent witness to the twisted game she and Callen had been forced to endure. Her fingers tightened around the hilt of her dagger, the weight of Callen's absence pressing heavily on her heart.

"Where is he?" she demanded again, her voice trembling with a mix of fury and desperation.

The Queen remained seated on her obsidian throne, her golden eyes glowing with cold amusement. She rested her chin on one hand, her fingers tapping idly against the armrest. "Callen is… elsewhere," she said, her voice lilting and serene. "He has his own truths to face, just as you do."

Evanna's heart clenched. "What does that mean? What have you done to him?"

The Queen's smile widened. "I've done nothing that he hasn't already done to himself. The Court merely reflects what lies within. Callen's struggle is his own, but whether he survives it is entirely up to him."

Evanna's hands trembled with the urge to lash out, but she forced herself to remain calm. The Queen thrived on chaos, on the unraveling of her opponents. Losing control would only give her more power.

"What do you want from me?" Evanna asked, her voice steady despite the turmoil roiling inside her.

The Queen tilted her head, her expression thoughtful. "You seek answers, do you not? About the Court, the Vale, and your place within it. Very well. I will give you a chance to find them." She gestured toward a doorway that had not been there moments before, its frame carved with intricate runes that pulsed faintly with golden light. "Beyond this door lies the Keeper of Truths. He holds the knowledge you seek, but be warned—truth is a double-edged sword. Once you see it, you cannot unsee it."

Evanna hesitated, her gaze shifting between the Queen and the glowing doorway. She didn't trust the Queen—she couldn't— but the chance to uncover the truth was too important to ignore.

If there was even a sliver of hope that the Keeper could help her find Callen and end the Queen's reign, she had to take it.

"I'm not afraid of the truth," she said, stepping toward the doorway.

The Queen's laughter followed her, soft and mocking. "Oh, my dear," she said, her voice fading as Evanna crossed the threshold. "You should be."

—-

The air beyond the doorway was thick and cold, carrying a faint metallic tang that stung Evanna's nostrils. The corridor stretched endlessly before her, its walls smooth and featureless, glowing faintly with a pale, silvery light. Her footsteps echoed eerily, each sound magnified as though the corridor itself were alive and listening.

The whispers returned, soft and indistinct at first, but growing louder with each step. They spoke in fragments, pieces of conversations that seemed both familiar and foreign. She heard her mother's voice, sharp with worry, mingling with Callen's, filled with pain and regret. Other voices joined the chorus, some she recognized, others she did not.

"You could have saved her…"
  "He's not who you think he is…"
  "You don't belong here…"

Evanna shook her head, trying to block out the voices, but they only grew louder. The corridor twisted and turned, each step taking her deeper into the labyrinthine space. The whispers pressed closer, wrapping around her like a suffocating veil.

Finally, she emerged into a circular chamber bathed in an ethereal glow. At its center stood a figure cloaked in tattered robes, its face obscured by a hood. The figure stood motionless, its hands clasped around a long staff carved with runes that glimmered faintly in the dim light.

"Are you the Keeper of Truths?" Evanna asked, her voice echoing in the silence.

The figure tilted its head, its movements slow and deliberate. When it spoke, its voice was deep and resonant, carrying an otherworldly weight that sent a shiver down her spine. "I am the Keeper," it said. "Seeker of truths, speaker of none. What do you seek, mortal?"

"I need to know how to stop the Queen," Evanna said, stepping closer. "How to break her hold on Callen—and on the Vale."

The Keeper was silent for a long moment, its hooded gaze fixed on her. "The truth you seek lies not in the Queen's power," it said finally. "It lies in the choices you have made—and the ones you have yet to make."

Evanna frowned, her frustration mounting. "What does that mean? I need real answers, not riddles."

The Keeper raised a hand, and the room shifted. The walls

dissolved into darkness, and the floor beneath her feet gave way to a swirling void. Evanna stumbled but managed to regain her footing as images began to coalesce in the air around her.

She saw herself as a child, standing at the edge of the Vale, her mother's voice calling her back. She saw Callen, his face twisted with anguish, as he knelt before the Queen. She saw the Queen herself, standing in a grand hall, her golden eyes gleaming with malice.

But then the images changed.

She saw Callen standing at the edge of a battlefield, his blade slick with blood. She saw a shadowy figure whispering in his ear, its form indistinct but its presence unmistakably sinister. She saw the Queen reaching out to him, her hand glowing with dark energy, as he hesitated, torn between defiance and submission.

"What is this?" Evanna demanded, her voice shaking.

"The truth," the Keeper said. "Callen's fall was not of the Queen's making. The shadows that bind him were born of his own choices—choices made in desperation and fear."

Evanna's heart ached as she watched the scenes unfold. She saw Callen turning away from the battlefield, his face lined with regret, as the shadowy figure vanished into the darkness. She saw him kneeling before the Queen, his head bowed, as the glowing markings appeared on his arm.

"He gave himself to her," the Keeper said. "Not out of loyalty, but out of despair. He sought to undo what could not be undone, and in doing so, he bound himself to her will."

Evanna shook her head, her mind reeling. "There has to be a way to break her hold," she said. "There has to be."

The Keeper was silent for a long moment before speaking again. "There is a way," it said. "But it comes at a cost."

"What cost?" Evanna asked, her voice trembling.

The Keeper raised its staff, and the images shifted once more. She saw herself standing before the Queen, her hands glowing with light as the shadows recoiled around her. She saw Callen at her side, his face etched with pain and determination. And she saw the shadows surging toward her, their forms twisting and writhing as they consumed everything in their path.

"To break the Queen's hold, you must face the shadows within yourself," the Keeper said. "Only then can you sever the ties that bind him—and the Vale."

Evanna's breath caught, the weight of the Keeper's words settling heavily on her chest. The path before her was clear, but it was one she was not certain she could walk.

"Will you take the truth, mortal?" the Keeper asked, its voice reverberating through the chamber. "Or will you turn away, as so many before you have?"

Evanna hesitated, her heart pounding. She thought of Callen, of her mother, of the countless lives that had been touched by the Queen's darkness. She thought of the choices she had made and the ones she had yet to make.

"I'll take it," she said finally, her voice steady. "I'll face the truth—no matter what it costs."

The Keeper lowered its staff, and the void around her dissolved into light. As the chamber faded away, Evanna felt a sense of resolve settle over her.

The path ahead was uncertain, but she was ready to face it. For Callen. For the Vale. And for the truth.

Fifteen

The Forbidden Heir

The chamber dissolved into a swirling haze of golden light and shadow, leaving Evanna suspended in a space that felt untethered from reality. The Keeper of Truths had vanished, but its final words lingered in her mind, heavy with implication: To sever the ties that bind him—and the Vale—you must face the shadows within yourself.

As the mist cleared, she found herself standing on the edge of a grand precipice, overlooking a sprawling, desolate landscape. The ground below was cracked and barren, veins of glowing crimson light snaking through the earth like molten rivers. In the distance, a towering fortress loomed against the horizon, its spires reaching toward the roiling, storm-filled sky. The sight of it sent a chill down her spine—this was no ordinary stronghold. This was the Queen's citadel, the heart of the Court of Endless Dusk.

Evanna steeled herself, gripping the hilt of her dagger as she stepped forward. The air here was thick with a palpable energy that seemed to vibrate through her very bones. Every instinct screamed at her to turn back, but she pushed forward, driven by the knowledge that Callen was somewhere within those walls.

—-

The path to the citadel was narrow and treacherous, winding through jagged cliffs and across rickety bridges that creaked ominously with every step. The closer she drew to the fortress, the heavier the air became, until it felt as though she were wading through an invisible tide. The whispers that had plagued her throughout the Vale returned, louder and more insistent than ever, their fragmented words clawing at the edges of her mind.

"You cannot save him…"
  "He belongs to her…"
  "You will fail…"

Evanna clenched her jaw, forcing herself to focus. The whispers were lies—she couldn't let them take hold.

The final bridge was the most perilous, its wooden planks warped and splintered with age. The wind howled around her as she crossed, the citadel's towering gates looming ever closer. With each step, her resolve hardened. She had come too far to turn back now.

—-

The gates were massive, carved from dark stone and etched with intricate runes that glowed faintly in the dim light. As she approached, the runes flared brightly, and the gates groaned open, revealing a vast courtyard shrouded in mist. The air here was even colder, and the oppressive energy of the Queen's presence was nearly suffocating.

Evanna stepped inside, her senses on high alert. The courtyard was eerily silent, save for the faint rustling of the mist as it swirled around her feet. Shadows danced along the edges of her vision, their movements quick and fleeting. She tightened her grip on her dagger, her heart pounding.

Suddenly, a voice rang out, sharp and commanding. "You shouldn't be here."

Evanna whirled around to find a figure standing in the center of the courtyard. It was a man, clad in dark, ornate armor that gleamed with an otherworldly light. His face was partially obscured by a helm, but his piercing blue eyes were unmistakable.

"Callen," she breathed, relief flooding through her.

But the relief was short-lived. There was something different about him—something cold and distant. The glowing markings on his arm were brighter than ever, pulsing in time with the runes on the gates. His stance was rigid, and his gaze was sharp and unyielding.

"Leave," he said, his voice devoid of emotion. "You don't belong here."

Evanna's stomach twisted. "Callen, it's me. It's Evanna. Don't you recognize me?"

He hesitated for a fraction of a second, his gaze flickering with something unspoken. But then his expression hardened, and he drew his blade. "I said leave."

Evanna took a step forward, her heart aching. "I'm not leaving without you."

—-

Callen's grip on his blade tightened, his knuckles white. "You don't understand. I'm bound to her. If you stay, she'll destroy you."

"She doesn't control you, Callen," Evanna said, her voice firm. "She only has the power you give her."

"You're wrong," he said, his tone sharp and bitter. "You don't know what I've done. The things I've sacrificed…"

"I don't care," Evanna interrupted, her eyes blazing with determination. "You're not hers. You never were."

Her words seemed to strike a chord, and for a moment, his resolve faltered. But then the shadows around them surged, coiling like living serpents, and the Queen's voice echoed through the courtyard.

"Ah, the healer," she said, her tone smooth and mocking. "So persistent. So foolish."

Evanna turned, her eyes narrowing as the Queen appeared at the far end of the courtyard. She moved with an unnatural grace, her golden eyes gleaming with malice. The shadows parted around her, as though they were drawn to her presence.

"You cannot save him," the Queen said, her gaze fixed on Evanna. "He belongs to me. Just as you will, soon enough."

Evanna raised her dagger, her hands trembling but steady. "I don't belong to you. And neither does he."

The Queen's laughter rang out, cold and sharp. "You think you can defy me? The Court is mine. The Vale is mine. Everything you see bends to my will."

"Not everything," Evanna shot back. "You're afraid of the truth. That's why you hide it, why you twist and manipulate it. But I've seen it now. I know your hold on him isn't unbreakable."

The Queen's expression darkened, her golden eyes narrowing. "You know nothing."

—-

Before Evanna could respond, the shadows surged forward, engulfing the courtyard in darkness. She braced herself, her dagger ready, but the attack never came. Instead, the shadows coalesced into a single figure—a young boy with dark hair and piercing blue eyes.

Evanna's breath caught as the boy stepped forward, his expression blank and emotionless. "Who... who is that?" she whispered.

The Queen's smile returned, cold and triumphant. "The heir to my throne," she said. "The rightful ruler of the Court of Endless Dusk. A child born of shadow and sacrifice. My creation."

Evanna's heart pounded as she looked at the boy, realization dawning. "He's... Callen?"

The Queen laughed. "No, my dear. He is what Callen was meant to be. The perfect vessel. The perfect servant. But Callen was weak. He faltered, and so I made another."

Evanna's blood ran cold. "You're lying."

"Am I?" the Queen said, her tone mocking. "Ask him yourself."

The boy stepped closer, his gaze locking onto Callen's. For a moment, the courtyard was silent, the tension thick enough to cut with a blade.

"You betrayed us," the boy said, his voice soft but filled with venom. "You turned away from your destiny."

Callen's hands trembled, his blade lowering. "I didn't... I didn't know."

"Enough," the Queen said sharply. "It is time to end this. Callen, kill her."

Evanna's heart ached as Callen turned toward her, his expression torn. The Queen's command hung in the air, a dark cloud of inevitability. But Evanna refused to back down.

"Callen," she said, her voice strong and steady. "You have a choice. You've always had a choice."

His blade wavered, his eyes flickering with anguish. The boy stepped closer, his presence a chilling reminder of what Callen had tried to escape.

And then, in that moment of stillness, Callen made his choice.

The shadows erupted, and the battle began.

Sixteen

The Edge of Oblivion

The shadows erupted in a chaotic storm, engulfing the courtyard in darkness so thick it swallowed the torches lining the walls. The only light came from the Queen's golden eyes, which gleamed with cold malice, and the faint, pulsing glow of the runes on Callen's arm. The air was alive with energy, crackling and hissing as the Queen's will manifested in every corner of the space.

Evanna barely had time to react before the first wave of shadows lunged toward her. They moved like serpents, fast and fluid, their forms shifting and twisting with unnatural grace. She dodged the attack, her dagger slicing through one of the shadowy tendrils, which dissipated with a sharp hiss. But more replaced it, each one more aggressive than the last.

"Callen!" she shouted, her voice strained. "Help me!"

But Callen stood frozen, his blade trembling in his hand. His face was pale, his eyes locked on the shadowy figure of the boy who stood at the Queen's side. The boy's presence was unnerving, his expression blank but his eyes filled with a cold, calculating intelligence far beyond his years.

"You were supposed to lead us," the boy said, his voice soft but cutting. "You were meant to be the one who carried the Queen's will. Instead, you turned your back on us. On me."

"I didn't know," Callen whispered, his voice barely audible. "I didn't know what she was doing."

"You knew," the boy countered, stepping closer. "You just didn't care."

The words struck Callen like a blow, and he staggered back, his blade slipping from his hand. Evanna's heart sank as she watched him falter, his inner battle playing out before her eyes. She turned back to the shadows, her resolve hardening.

—-

The Queen watched the scene unfold with an air of satisfaction, her hands clasped in front of her as though she were merely observing a game. "This is the beauty of the Court," she said, her voice smooth and serene. "Truth and lies, light and shadow—all are intertwined. You cannot escape it, healer. And neither can he."

Evanna gritted her teeth, her dagger flashing as she fought

off another wave of shadows. "You don't control us," she spat. "We're not yours."

The Queen's laughter rang out, cold and mocking. "Oh, my dear, you misunderstand. The Court doesn't need to control you. It merely reveals what was already there."

As if to prove her point, the shadows around Evanna shifted, forming into familiar shapes. She froze as the figures of her mother and Callen emerged from the darkness, their faces twisted with anger and accusation.

"You let me die," her mother said, her voice filled with venom. "You weren't strong enough to save me," Callen added, his tone laced with disappointment.

Evanna's chest tightened, the weight of their words pressing down on her like a physical force. "You're not real," she said, her voice trembling. "You're not real!"

The figures stepped closer, their eyes burning with an unnatural light. "You failed us," they said in unison. "You always fail."

—-

"Evanna, don't listen to them!" Callen's voice cut through the chaos, sharp and desperate.

She turned toward him, her vision blurring with unshed tears. He had picked up his blade and was charging toward her, his glowing markings flaring brightly as he cut through the shadows that surrounded her. The figures of her mother and Callen dissipated, their voices fading into the ether.

"You can't let her get to you," he said, grabbing her arm and pulling her to her feet. "That's how she wins."

Evanna nodded, her grip on her dagger tightening. "We have to stop her," she said. "We have to end this."

Callen's jaw tightened, his gaze shifting to the Queen. "We will."

—-

The Queen raised a hand, and the shadows around her coalesced into a massive, towering form. It was a creature of pure darkness, its body shifting and writhing like a storm cloud. Its eyes glowed with a fiery red light, and its jagged claws gleamed like polished obsidian.

"Face the Harbinger," the Queen said, her tone almost gleeful. "Let it judge your worth."

The Harbinger let out a deafening roar, the sound reverberating through the courtyard like a physical force. It lunged at Evanna and Callen, its claws slicing through the air with terrifying speed.

Callen pushed Evanna out of the way, raising his blade to block the attack. The impact sent him stumbling back, but he managed to hold his ground. The glowing markings on his arm flared even brighter, and he gritted his teeth as he pushed back against the creature's overwhelming strength.

"Evanna!" he shouted. "I can't hold it off alone!"

Evanna scrambled to her feet, her mind racing. The Harbinger was too powerful to face head-on, but there had to be a way to weaken it. Her gaze flickered to the Queen, who stood watching with a smug expression.

"It's tied to her," Evanna realized, her voice barely audible. "If we can break her focus, we can weaken it."

Callen nodded, his expression grim. "Then do it. I'll keep it distracted."

—-

Evanna darted toward the Queen, her movements swift and precise. The shadows around her surged, but she cut through them with her dagger, her determination outweighing her fear. The Queen watched her approach, her golden eyes narrowing.

"You think you can challenge me, healer?" she said, her tone laced with disdain. "You are nothing but a pawn in a game far greater than you."

"Maybe," Evanna said, her voice steady. "But even pawns can take down a queen."

The Queen's smile faltered, and for the first time, a flicker of uncertainty crossed her face. Evanna seized the moment, raising her dagger and plunging it into the ground at the Queen's feet. The blade glowed brightly, its light spreading outward in a ripple of energy that disrupted the shadows.

The Harbinger let out a pained roar, its form flickering and distorting as the Queen's connection to it weakened. Callen took advantage of the opening, driving his blade into the creature's chest. The Harbinger shattered into a cloud of darkness, its pieces dissolving into the air.

—-

The Queen staggered, her golden eyes blazing with fury. "You dare defy me?" she hissed, her voice echoing with a terrible power.

Evanna stepped forward, her dagger still glowing with the light of her defiance. "You've ruled through fear and manipulation for long enough," she said. "Your time is over."

The Queen raised her hand, the shadows surging around her like a tidal wave. But before she could strike, Callen appeared at Evanna's side, his glowing markings casting a brilliant light that cut through the darkness.

Together, they stood against the Queen, their combined resolve shining like a beacon in the heart of the Court. The shadows recoiled, their power waning in the face of their defiance.

"You cannot win," the Queen snarled, her voice trembling with rage.

"Maybe not," Evanna said, her gaze unwavering. "But we can try."

And with that, they charged, the light of their determination piercing through the darkness. The battle for the Court—and for their souls—had truly begun.

Seventeen

The Queen's Gambit

The Court of Endless Dusk was in chaos. The ground beneath Evanna and Callen trembled with each step as they moved closer to the obsidian throne, the very fabric of the Queen's domain rebelling against their defiance. Shadows twisted and writhed around them, some lunging to attack while others retreated, as though unsure of how to respond to the radiant glow emanating from Callen's markings and the light pulsing from Evanna's dagger.

The Queen stood before her throne, her golden eyes burning with fury. Her hands were raised, her fingers weaving intricate patterns in the air as she summoned the full power of the Court. The shadows surged at her command, forming a vortex of darkness that filled the hall with an ear-piercing roar.

"You think you can challenge me?" she spat, her voice resonating with an unnatural echo. "I am the Court! I am the Vale! You are nothing but ants scurrying beneath my feet."

Evanna tightened her grip on her glowing dagger, her heart pounding as she exchanged a glance with Callen. "We've come this far," she said, her voice steady despite the fear threatening to overwhelm her. "We can't back down now."

Callen nodded, his blade shimmering with the light of the markings on his arm. "Whatever happens, we face her together."

—-

The Queen's vortex of shadows exploded outward, and Evanna and Callen were forced to dive in opposite directions to avoid the onslaught. The tendrils of darkness slammed into the walls of the hall, shattering stone and sending shards raining down like deadly hail.

Evanna rolled to her feet, her eyes darting around the room as she searched for Callen. She spotted him near the base of the throne, his blade raised as he slashed through a wave of shadowy figures that had emerged from the vortex. His movements were precise and deliberate, his glowing markings flaring with each strike.

But the Queen was far from finished. With a flick of her wrist, she summoned another surge of shadows, this one forming into a massive, serpentine creature with eyes that burned like coals. The creature hissed, its long body coiling as it lunged toward Callen.

"Callen!" Evanna shouted, sprinting toward him.

Callen turned just in time to see the creature's attack. He raised his blade, the glowing markings on his arm flaring as he parried the strike. The force of the impact sent him stumbling back, but he quickly regained his footing, his gaze locked on the monstrous serpent.

"Go for the Queen!" he yelled to Evanna, his voice strained. "I'll handle this!"

Evanna hesitated for only a moment before nodding. She turned her attention to the Queen, who watched the battle unfold with a cruel smile. Evanna's heart burned with determination as she charged forward, her glowing dagger slicing through the tendrils of shadow that rose to block her path.

—-

The Queen raised a hand, and the shadows around her solidified into a barrier of dark, jagged spikes. "You are bold, healer," she said, her tone mocking. "But your defiance is meaningless. The Court does not fall to mortals."

Evanna's dagger pulsed with light as she slashed at the barrier, her strikes carving glowing fissures into the dark surface. "The Court falls when it overreaches," she retorted, her voice steady. "Your power is built on fear, and fear can be broken."

The Queen's smile faltered for a fraction of a second, and Evanna seized the opportunity. She drove her dagger into the barrier with all her strength, shattering it in a burst of light. The Queen staggered back, her golden eyes narrowing as Evanna closed the distance between them.

"You are stronger than I anticipated," the Queen admitted, her voice cold. "But strength alone will not save you."

She raised her hands, and the shadows around her coalesced into a series of bladed tendrils that lashed out at Evanna. Evanna dodged and weaved, her dagger flashing as she deflected the attacks. Each strike sent a jolt of pain through her arm, but she gritted her teeth and pressed on, determined to reach the Queen.

—-

Meanwhile, Callen continued his battle with the shadow serpent. The creature was relentless, its attacks swift and deadly. Callen's glowing markings flared with each strike, his blade slicing through the serpent's coiling form, but the creature regenerated almost instantly, its shadowy body reforming with each blow.

"You can't fight her forever," the serpent hissed, its voice a low, menacing rumble. "She will consume you, as she consumes all."

Callen ignored the taunt, his focus unyielding. He dodged another strike, his blade cutting through the serpent's head. For a brief moment, the creature dissolved into a cloud of shadow, and Callen took the opportunity to sprint toward the throne, his gaze locked on the Queen.

—-

Evanna and Callen converged on the Queen at the same time, their movements perfectly synchronized. Evanna's dagger glowed with blinding light as she lunged at the Queen, while Callen's blade shimmered with the energy of his markings. Together, they struck, their weapons aimed directly at the Queen's heart.

But at the last moment, the Queen vanished, her form dissolving into shadows. Evanna and Callen stumbled forward, their strikes hitting nothing but empty air.

The Queen reappeared at the top of the throne, her golden eyes blazing with fury. "You are more troublesome than I expected," she said, her voice dripping with venom. "But this game is far from over."

She raised her hands, and the entire hall began to tremble. The shadows around her surged upward, forming a massive, swirling storm that threatened to consume everything in its path.

"Evanna!" Callen shouted, grabbing her arm. "We have to stop her now!"

Evanna nodded, her gaze locking onto the Queen. Together, they sprinted toward the throne, their weapons glowing with a light that cut through the encroaching darkness.

—-

The final confrontation was chaos. The Queen unleashed everything she had, the shadows lashing out in a storm of unrelenting fury. Evanna and Callen fought side by side, their movements perfectly coordinated as they cut through the waves of darkness. The glow of their weapons illuminated the hall, their light pushing back against the Queen's encroaching storm.

"You cannot win!" the Queen roared, her voice reverberating through the chamber. "The Court is eternal!"

Evanna's eyes blazed with determination as she lunged at the Queen, her dagger slicing through the storm. "Nothing is eternal," she said, her voice steady. "Not even you."

With a final, desperate strike, she drove her dagger into the Queen's chest. The blade pulsed with light, and for a moment, time seemed to stand still.

The Queen let out a scream, her form dissolving into a torrent of shadows that swirled around the throne. The storm collapsed in on itself, and the hall was filled with blinding light.

When the light faded, the Queen was gone, and the shadows had vanished. The hall was silent, save for the sound of Evanna and Callen's ragged breathing.

—-

Callen sank to his knees, his glowing markings dimming as he stared at the empty throne. "Is it over?" he asked, his voice trembling.

Evanna knelt beside him, her dagger still glowing faintly. "I think so," she said, her voice soft.

The weight of their victory settled over them, and for the first time, they allowed themselves to hope. The Queen's gambit had failed, and the Court of Endless Dusk had been shattered.

But as they stood in the ruins of the throne room, a faint whisper echoed through the air, chilling them to the bone: The shadows always return.

Eighteen

The Heir's Awakening

The throne room was unnervingly silent after the Queen's defeat, the echoes of her final scream still lingering in the cold, stagnant air. The shadows that had once writhed and coiled with a life of their own now lay still, their oppressive weight lifted. But the eerie quiet felt less like a victory and more like the eye of a storm, the kind of stillness that promised something darker yet to come.

Evanna stood beside Callen near the shattered remnants of the obsidian throne. Her dagger, still faintly glowing, hung loosely in her hand as her mind churned with questions. The Queen was gone—or so it seemed—but her presence still lingered, woven into the very stones of the Court. The weight of that realization pressed down on her as she turned to Callen, who knelt with his head bowed, the glow of his markings dim and flickering.

"Callen," she said softly, her voice cutting through the oppressive silence. "It's over. We stopped her."

Callen didn't respond. His gaze was fixed on the floor, his hands trembling as they gripped the hilt of his blade. Evanna stepped closer, concern tightening her chest. "Callen?" she repeated, kneeling beside him.

"I can still feel her," he murmured, his voice barely audible. "She's gone, but she's not… gone. It's like she left a piece of herself behind."

Evanna's stomach twisted. "What do you mean?"

Callen looked up, his eyes filled with a mixture of fear and anguish. "The Vale. The shadows. The Court itself. They're not tied to her—they're tied to me."

—-

Evanna's breath caught, her mind racing as she tried to make sense of his words. "No," she said, shaking her head. "That's not possible. You fought her. You broke free."

Callen's gaze turned distant, his jaw tightening. "I thought I did," he said. "But the truth is, I was always her vessel. Her pawn. Even when I thought I was defying her, I was still playing her game."

"Callen, stop," Evanna said, her voice firm. "You're not her pawn. You're not her anything. You made your own choices—your own sacrifices. That's what matters."

Before he could respond, a low rumble shook the throne room, the sound reverberating through the stones beneath their feet. The faint glow of the runes etched into the walls flared, their light flickering like dying embers. Evanna and Callen both rose to their feet, their gazes snapping to the far end of the room.

There, where the Queen had once stood, the shadows began to shift. They coalesced into a swirling vortex, dark and menacing, their movements erratic and violent. From the heart of the vortex came a voice—soft, childlike, and yet filled with a chilling, unnatural power.

"You cannot stop what was always meant to be."

Evanna's blood ran cold as a figure emerged from the vortex. It was the boy—the shadowy child who had confronted Callen during their battle with the Queen. His dark hair was tousled, his pale skin flawless, and his piercing blue eyes gleamed with an intelligence far beyond his years. But there was something different about him now. He no longer seemed like an extension of the Queen's will. He stood with an aura of authority, his presence commanding and undeniable.

"The heir," Callen whispered, his voice trembling.

Evanna's grip on her dagger tightened as she stepped protectively in front of Callen. "What do you want?" she demanded, her voice steady despite the fear clawing at her chest.

The boy smiled, a cold, calculated expression that sent a shiver down her spine. "To reclaim what is mine," he said simply. "The Queen is gone, but her power remains. And now, it belongs to me."

—-

The room trembled again as the boy raised his hand, the shadows surging forward to encircle him like a living crown. The faint light of the runes was snuffed out, plunging the throne room into darkness save for the eerie glow of the boy's eyes and the faint, flickering light of Evanna's dagger.

"You've seen what the Court is capable of," the boy continued, his voice calm and measured. "Its power. Its reach. The Queen was only the beginning. Under my rule, the Court will rise to heights she never imagined."

"We won't let that happen," Evanna said, her voice defiant.

The boy tilted his head, his expression almost amused. "Won't you? You can barely stand, healer. And your companion…" His gaze shifted to Callen, who flinched under the weight of his stare. "He is already mine."

Callen clenched his fists, the glow of his markings flickering erratically. "I'm not yours," he said through gritted teeth. "I'll never be yours."

The boy stepped closer, his eyes narrowing. "You don't understand, do you? You were created for this. Your strength, your connection to the shadows—it all exists for one purpose: to serve the Court. To serve me."

—-

Callen staggered back, his hands clutching his head as though trying to block out the boy's words. Evanna moved to his side, her heart aching at the sight of his pain. "Don't listen to him," she said, her voice urgent. "You're stronger than this."

"Am I?" Callen's voice was strained, his body trembling. "What if he's right? What if I'm just another pawn in this game?"

"You're not," Evanna said firmly, grabbing his shoulders and forcing him to meet her gaze. "You're more than what she made you. You're more than what he says you are. You've fought too hard to give up now."

The boy watched the exchange with a faint smile, his eyes glinting with cruel amusement. "Touching," he said. "But words won't save him. The Court's power flows through his veins, and no amount of defiance can change that."

Evanna turned to face the boy, her dagger raised. "Then I'll cut that power out of him," she said, her voice steady. "Even if it means destroying you."

The boy's smile faded, his expression darkening. "You think you can kill me, healer? I am the Court now. I am its past, its present, and its future. You cannot destroy what is eternal."

"Maybe not," Evanna said. "But I can try."

—-

The boy raised his hand, and the shadows surged toward them like a tidal wave. Evanna and Callen braced themselves, their weapons glowing as they stood side by side. The impact was deafening, the force of the shadows slamming into them like a physical blow. But they held their ground, their combined light pushing back against the encroaching darkness.

"You are stubborn," the boy said, his voice filled with irritation. "But even stubbornness has its limits."

Evanna gritted her teeth, her dagger flaring with light as she slashed through the shadows. "And power has its flaws," she countered. "You're not invincible. None of you are."

The boy's eyes narrowed, his expression twisting with rage. He raised both hands, and the shadows coalesced into a massive, towering form—a monstrous creature of darkness with glowing red eyes and jagged claws.

"Then let's see how far your defiance takes you," the boy said.

The creature roared, its voice shaking the very foundations of the throne room. It lunged at them, its claws slicing through the air with deadly precision. Evanna and Callen moved as one, their weapons flashing as they dodged and countered its attacks.

The battle was chaos, the throne room filled with the sounds of clashing light and shadow. Evanna's heart pounded as she fought, her mind racing with the realization that this was no ordinary fight. The boy wasn't just a child wielding the Queen's power—he was something far more dangerous.

He was the future of the Court.

And unless they stopped him, he would destroy everything.

—-

As the battle raged on, Evanna's determination burned brighter than ever. She knew the stakes. She knew the odds. But she also knew that they couldn't afford to lose.

Together, she and Callen would face the darkness.

And together, they would bring the light.

Nineteen

Battle at Endless Dusk

The throne room erupted into chaos as the massive shadow beast lunged, its monstrous form twisting unnaturally as it bore down on Evanna and Callen. Its claws, sharp as obsidian blades, slashed through the air with a sound like tearing metal, sending cracks spidering across the stone floor wherever they struck.

Evanna rolled to the side, narrowly avoiding a devastating blow. Her heart pounded in her chest, the weight of her glowing dagger strangely reassuring as she tightened her grip. The light from her blade illuminated the encroaching shadows, each pulse driving them back momentarily before they surged forward again.

Callen stood a few feet away, his blade glowing faintly with the energy of his markings. He faced the beast head-on, his jaw clenched and his stance firm despite the overwhelming force bearing down on them. "We can't fight it like this!" he shouted over the deafening roar of the beast. "The shadows are feeding it. We have to weaken its connection to the Court."

Evanna's mind raced as she dodged another strike, the creature's claws raking through the air so close she felt the chill of their passage. The boy, the self-proclaimed heir to the Court, stood at the edge of the room, watching with a calm, calculated expression. His eyes gleamed with an unnatural light, his hands raised as if conducting the shadows like a symphony.

"He's controlling it!" Evanna yelled, pointing toward the boy. "If we disrupt his focus, it'll weaken the beast!"

Callen nodded, his gaze locking onto the boy. "Then we split up. I'll keep the beast distracted. You go after him."

Evanna hesitated for only a moment before nodding. "Be careful," she said, her voice laced with urgency.

"You too," Callen replied, his blade raised as he charged the shadow beast.

—-

Callen's attack was precise and relentless, his glowing blade carving through the creature's shadowy form. Each strike sent ripples of light through the beast, momentarily disrupting its shape before it reformed, stronger and angrier than before. The room trembled under the force of their clash, the air thick with the raw energy of their battle.

Meanwhile, Evanna sprinted toward the boy, her dagger glowing brighter with each step. The shadows around him writhed like living things, rising to block her path, but she slashed through them with determined precision. Her every movement was fueled by the knowledge that the boy's connection to the Court was the key to ending this battle.

The boy's calm demeanor faltered as Evanna drew closer. His piercing blue eyes narrowed, and he raised one hand, summoning a wall of shadows to separate them. Evanna didn't slow, her dagger flashing as she cut through the barrier, her resolve burning brighter than ever.

"You think you can stop me?" the boy sneered, his voice cold and sharp. "The Court is eternal. Its power flows through me now."

Evanna's dagger struck the ground at his feet, sending a shockwave of light through the room. The boy stumbled, his connection to the shadows flickering momentarily. "The Court may be eternal," she said, her voice steady, "but you're not."

—-

The shadow beast let out a deafening roar, its form faltering as the boy's control wavered. Callen seized the opportunity, driving his blade deep into the creature's chest. The glowing markings on his arm flared brightly, and the beast recoiled, its massive body writhing in agony.

"Evanna, whatever you're doing, keep going!" Callen shouted, his voice strained.

Evanna didn't hesitate. She lunged at the boy, her dagger slicing through the air as she aimed for the source of his power. But the boy was quick, his form blurring as he darted out of reach. His hands moved in a flurry of gestures, and the shadows around him surged, forming into sharp, jagged spikes that shot toward Evanna.

She ducked and rolled, her movements fluid as she dodged the attack. The spikes shattered against the floor, leaving behind deep gouges in the stone. Evanna's breath came in ragged gasps, but she refused to back down. She rose to her feet, her gaze locking onto the boy.

"You don't have to do this," she said, her voice steady but pleading. "The Queen is gone. You don't have to follow in her footsteps."

The boy's expression twisted into one of rage. "You don't understand," he hissed. "I am the Court. Without me, the shadows would consume everything. I am its balance, its order."

Evanna shook her head, her heart aching at the pain in his voice. "You're not balance—you're fear. And fear doesn't have to control you."

—-

The boy hesitated, his eyes flickering with uncertainty. For a moment, the shadows around him stilled, their movements less aggressive. But the reprieve was short-lived. The boy's expression hardened, and the shadows surged again, coiling around him like a protective barrier.

"Enough!" he shouted, his voice echoing with unnatural power. "If you won't submit, then you'll be consumed!"

The room darkened as the shadows closed in, their tendrils reaching for Evanna. She raised her dagger, its light flaring brightly as she slashed through the encroaching darkness. The glow of her weapon burned away the shadows, but she could feel their weight pressing against her, threatening to overwhelm her.

From the corner of her eye, she saw Callen battling the shadow beast with everything he had. His movements were slower now, his strength waning as the beast's attacks grew more ferocious. She knew they couldn't keep this up much longer.

Desperation fueled her next move. She gripped her dagger tightly and charged the boy, her blade cutting through the shadows as she closed the distance between them. He raised his hands to defend himself, but Evanna was faster. Her dagger struck his chest, the light of its blade flaring brightly as it pierced through the shadows.

The boy let out a cry of pain, his form flickering as the shadows around him unraveled. The shadow beast let out a final, guttural roar before collapsing into a cloud of darkness that dissipated into the air. The room fell silent, save for the sound of Evanna's ragged breathing and Callen's heavy footsteps as he approached.

—-

The boy crumpled to the ground, his small form trembling as the shadows withdrew. His piercing blue eyes looked up at Evanna, filled with a mixture of anger and despair. "You don't understand," he whispered, his voice broken. "Without the Court, there will be nothing."

Evanna knelt beside him, her dagger dimming as she placed a hand on his shoulder. "There can be something else," she said gently. "Something better. But you have to let go."

The boy's expression softened, his gaze searching hers for a long moment. Then, slowly, he nodded. The shadows around him dissipated completely, leaving the room bathed in a soft, golden light.

Callen knelt beside them, his glowing markings fading as he placed a hand on the boy's other shoulder. "You're not alone," he said, his voice quiet but firm. "We'll figure this out together."

The boy looked between them, his eyes filling with tears. "I'm… I'm sorry," he said, his voice trembling. "I didn't know how to stop."

"It's okay," Evanna said, her heart aching with relief. "It's over now."

—-

The three of them sat in the stillness of the throne room, the echoes of the battle fading into the distance. The Court of Endless Dusk had fallen, its grip on the Vale shattered. But as Evanna looked at the boy and Callen, she knew their journey was far from over.

They had won the battle, but the fight for the future had only just begun.

Twenty

Love and Sacrifice

The golden light that bathed the ruins of the throne room dimmed as the moments of stillness dragged on. Evanna, Callen, and the boy sat on the cracked stone floor, their breathing uneven, the silence around them thick with unspoken truths. The shadowy presence that had permeated the Court was gone, leaving behind a hollow emptiness that felt unnatural, like a wound in the fabric of reality.

Callen's gaze was fixed on the boy, whose frail form trembled with exhaustion. The shadows no longer surrounded him, but the air still carried the faintest trace of their power, as though they lingered just out of reach, waiting for the right moment to return.

"Are you hurt?" Callen asked, his voice low but steady.

The boy shook his head, his piercing blue eyes dull with weariness. "I'm fine," he murmured. "But the Court... it's breaking. Without her, it's falling apart."

Evanna's chest tightened. She had felt it too—the shifting energy beneath their feet, the faint tremors that vibrated through the stones. The Queen's defeat had severed the Court's anchor to the Vale, leaving it unstable, like a collapsing house of cards.

"How long do we have?" she asked, her voice calm but tinged with urgency.

The boy hesitated, his small hands clenching into fists. "Not long. The Court was tied to her will. Without it, everything here will dissolve... including us."

—-

Callen pushed himself to his feet, his blade still in hand, though its glow had dimmed to a faint shimmer. He turned to Evanna, his expression resolute. "We need to leave," he said. "Now."

Evanna stood as well, though her mind raced with questions. "And go where? The Court may be breaking, but the shadows will spread if we don't stop them. This isn't just about us—it's about the Vale."

Callen's jaw tightened, and he looked away, his hands trembling. "I know. But what choice do we have? The Queen's gone. The boy isn't controlling the shadows anymore. What else can we do?"

Evanna opened her mouth to respond, but before she could speak, the boy stood, his small frame radiating a quiet determination. "There is a way," he said softly, his voice cutting through the tension like a blade.

Both Evanna and Callen turned to him, their gazes sharp. "What do you mean?" Evanna asked.

The boy hesitated, his eyes flickering with fear and resolve. "The Court's power isn't entirely gone. It's… inside me. I can feel it, even now. If I take it back—if I become its anchor—I can stop the collapse."

Callen's eyes widened, and he shook his head vehemently. "No. That's not an option. You're just a kid. You've already been through enough."

The boy met Callen's gaze, his expression unwavering. "I may be a child, but I was made for this," he said. "The Court is a part of me, whether I like it or not. If I take it back, I can stabilize it. I can keep the shadows contained."

"At what cost?" Evanna asked, her voice trembling. She already knew the answer, but she needed to hear it spoken aloud.

The boy's shoulders sagged, and he looked down at his hands. "If I do this… I won't be me anymore. I'll become the Court. A vessel for its power. I'll never leave this place."

—-

Silence fell over the room as the weight of his words settled over them. Evanna's heart ached as she looked at the boy, his small frame bearing the weight of a burden no one should have to carry. She glanced at Callen, whose face was etched with anguish and guilt.

"There has to be another way," Callen said, his voice breaking. "We just need more time to figure it out."

"There isn't time," the boy said firmly. "The longer we wait, the worse it will get. You've seen what the shadows can do. If they spread unchecked, they'll consume everything."

Evanna felt tears prick at her eyes, but she forced them back, her hands clenching into fists. "You can't do this alone," she said. "If you're going to take the power back, we'll find a way to share the burden. We'll stand with you."

The boy shook his head, a sad smile tugging at his lips. "It doesn't work that way," he said. "The Court needs one anchor— one soul to bind its power. It has to be me."

Callen stepped forward, his glowing markings flaring faintly as he placed a hand on the boy's shoulder. "You don't have to do this," he said, his voice trembling. "You've already given so much. Let us find another way."

The boy looked up at him, his expression filled with both pain and gratitude. "You gave me a choice," he said softly. "No one else ever did. And this is the choice I'm making."

—-

The tremors beneath their feet grew stronger, the walls of the throne room cracking as the Court continued to unravel. The golden light dimmed further, casting the room in a somber, flickering glow.

Evanna stepped forward, her heart breaking as she knelt before the boy. "If this is your choice," she said, her voice steady despite the tears streaming down her face, "then we'll honor it. But you need to know—you're not doing this alone. We'll stay with you until the end."

The boy's eyes filled with tears, and he nodded, his small hands reaching out to grasp hers. "Thank you," he whispered. "For everything."

Callen knelt beside them, his hand resting on the boy's shoulder. "You're braver than any of us," he said quietly. "Don't ever forget that."

—-

The boy took a deep breath, his expression resolute as he stepped toward the center of the room. The air around him seemed to hum with energy, the faint remnants of the Court's power coalescing around him like a cloak. He raised his arms, his voice steady as he began to speak words in a language neither Evanna nor Callen could understand.

The room erupted with light, a blinding, golden radiance that filled every corner of the space. The walls trembled, and the ground beneath their feet cracked and buckled as the power of the Court surged toward the boy, drawn to him like a moth to a flame.

Evanna and Callen shielded their eyes, their hearts pounding as the light grew brighter and brighter. The boy stood at the center of it all, his small frame radiating an otherworldly strength as he absorbed the Court's power.

And then, as suddenly as it began, the light faded.

—-

When Evanna opened her eyes, the throne room was empty. The cracks in the walls had disappeared, the tremors had ceased, and the oppressive weight of the shadows was gone. The air was still, and for the first time in what felt like an eternity, there was peace.

But the boy was gone.

Evanna fell to her knees, her chest heaving with sobs as the reality of his sacrifice washed over her. Callen stood silently beside her, his hands clenched into fists as tears streamed down his face.

"He did it," Evanna whispered, her voice breaking. "He saved us."

Callen nodded, his gaze distant. "He gave everything."

They sat in the quiet, their hearts heavy with grief and gratitude. The boy's sacrifice had saved the Vale, but it had come at a cost they would carry forever.

Love and sacrifice had won the battle, but the scars it left behind would never truly heal.

Twenty-One

A Kingdom Reborn

The silence that followed the boy's sacrifice was unlike anything Evanna had ever experienced. It wasn't the oppressive stillness of the Court of Endless Dusk, but something softer, more profound—a silence filled with the weight of loss and the promise of something new. The air was lighter now, the shadows no longer writhing and alive but resting quietly in the corners, as though the Court itself were holding its breath.

Evanna knelt in the center of the throne room, her hand resting on the cold stone where the boy had stood only moments before. The golden light that had marked his ascension to the Court's anchor had faded, leaving behind a faint glow that lingered in the air like a memory. She traced the cracks in the floor with her fingers, her heart heavy with the enormity of what he had done.

"He gave us a second chance," Callen said softly, his voice breaking the silence. He stood a few feet away, his glowing markings dim but steady, a testament to the boy's final act of stabilizing the Court. "We can't let it go to waste."

Evanna looked up at him, her eyes rimmed with tears. "What happens now?" she asked, her voice trembling. "The shadows are still here. The Court is still here. How do we make sure this doesn't happen again?"

Callen hesitated, his gaze distant as he considered her question. "The Queen's power is gone," he said finally. "The boy took it with him. The Court is… different now. It's not tied to her will, but it still exists. It always will."

Evanna's stomach churned at the thought. "So, it could happen again? Someone could take control, like she did?"

"Not if we don't let them," Callen said, his voice firm. "The Court is a part of the Vale. It's always been here, in one form or another. It doesn't have to be a force of destruction. Maybe it can be something else—something better."

—-

As they spoke, the throne room began to change. The jagged cracks in the walls smoothed over, the dark stone softening into a warm, pearlescent gray. The oppressive air lightened, and the faint glow of the runes that lined the room took on a softer, more natural hue. The throne itself, once a twisted mass of obsidian, shifted into a simple yet elegant seat carved from pale stone.

Evanna watched in awe as the transformation unfolded around them. The shadows that had once dominated the Court receded further, their movements slow and languid, as though they were content to rest. The room felt alive, but no longer hostile. It was as if the Court were breathing again, finding a new balance in the wake of its rebirth.

"Did he do this?" she asked, her voice hushed.

Callen nodded, his expression somber. "The boy didn't just stabilize the Court. He remade it. This is his legacy—a place that reflects what it could have been, instead of what the Queen turned it into."

Evanna felt a pang of sorrow at the thought of the boy, gone but not forgotten. "He gave everything for this," she said softly. "How do we honor that?"

—-

Callen stepped forward, his gaze fixed on the transformed throne. "We protect it," he said. "We make sure no one uses the Court's power the way the Queen did. We guard it, not as rulers, but as caretakers."

Evanna hesitated, her heart heavy with doubt. "But what about the Vale? The people? How do we explain this to them? How do we make them understand?"

Callen turned to her, his eyes steady. "We start by telling the truth," he said. "About the Queen, about the Court, and about the boy who saved us all. We can't erase what happened, but we can make sure it doesn't happen again."

Evanna nodded slowly, her resolve hardening. She thought of the people of the Vale, their lives touched by the shadows in ways they might never fully understand. They deserved to know the truth—to understand the sacrifices that had been made for them.

—-

The floor beneath their feet trembled softly, and a low hum filled the air. Evanna and Callen turned as a figure emerged from the shadows at the far end of the room. It was tall and humanoid, its form composed entirely of faint, shimmering light. It moved with a slow, deliberate grace, its presence both otherworldly and strangely comforting.

"What is that?" Evanna whispered, her voice tinged with awe.

Callen's eyes widened as he stepped closer. "I think… it's him."

The figure stopped a few feet away, its glowing form shifting faintly as it regarded them. When it spoke, its voice was soft and familiar, echoing with the boy's tone but layered with something deeper, something timeless.

"The Court has been reborn," the figure said. "Its purpose is no longer to serve the will of one, but to safeguard the balance of many. You are its guardians now."

Evanna's breath caught in her throat. "You mean… us?"

The figure nodded. "The shadows are not your enemies. They are a part of the Vale, just as you are. They need guidance, not control. You must protect them, and in doing so, protect the people of the Vale."

Callen stepped forward, his voice steady. "We'll do it," he said. "We'll make sure the Court serves its true purpose."

The figure's light flared briefly, as though in acknowledgment. "The path ahead will not be easy," it said. "But you are not alone. The Court is with you, and so am I."

Evanna felt tears prick at her eyes. "Thank you," she whispered. "For everything."

The figure inclined its head, its form beginning to fade. "Remember," it said, its voice growing faint. "Love and sacrifice are the foundations of the Vale. Never forget what was given to make this possible."

With those final words, the figure dissolved into the air, leaving behind a faint, lingering warmth that filled the room.

—-

For a long moment, Evanna and Callen stood in silence, their hearts heavy with the weight of their new responsibility. The throne room, now transformed into a place of light and calm, felt both welcoming and humbling.

"What now?" Evanna asked, her voice barely above a whisper.

Callen turned to her, his expression resolute. "Now, we rebuild," he said. "For the Vale. For the boy. For everyone."

Evanna nodded, her resolve hardening. Together, they would honor the boy's sacrifice by ensuring that the Court of Endless Dusk became a force for good—a beacon of hope in a world that had seen too much darkness.

As they left the throne room and stepped into the Vale, the first rays of dawn broke over the horizon, casting the land in a soft, golden light. It was a new day—a new beginning—and they were ready to face it.

The kingdom had been reborn, and with it, a chance to forge a brighter future.

Twenty-Two

The Dusk Eternal

The Vale was quiet in the days that followed the Court's rebirth. The oppressive shadows that had once loomed over the land had receded, leaving the skies a deep, twilight hue that seemed to stretch endlessly. The sun had not returned, but the perpetual dusk carried a strange peace—neither the blinding brightness of day nor the choking darkness of night. It was a delicate balance, fragile yet serene.

Evanna and Callen stood on the edge of a cliff overlooking the Vale, their gazes sweeping across the transformed landscape. The Court of Endless Dusk loomed in the distance, its towering spires softened by the faint glow of the sky. The jagged edges of its walls had smoothed into elegant curves, and the oppressive energy that had once surrounded it was now a quiet hum of power—calm but watchful.

"It feels... different," Evanna said softly, her voice barely carrying over the faint breeze. "Like it's holding its breath."

"It's alive," Callen replied, his glowing markings faint but steady. "The Court isn't just a place—it's a part of the Vale, just like the land and the people. It feels us, just as we feel it."

Evanna's heart ached as she thought of the boy, the one who had given everything to bring this balance. His sacrifice had stabilized the Court, but it had also left a void—one that Evanna wasn't sure they could ever truly fill.

—-

Their descent into the Vale was quiet, the air around them heavy with the weight of unspoken truths. The people of the villages had begun to emerge from their homes, their faces etched with confusion and wariness. They had felt the shift in the Vale, the strange stillness that had replaced the shadows, but they didn't yet understand what it meant.

As Evanna and Callen entered the first village, they were met with a mixture of hope and fear. The villagers gathered cautiously, their eyes darting to the glowing markings on Callen's arm and the faint shimmer of Evanna's dagger. Whispers rippled through the crowd, soft and uncertain.

"They were in the Court..."
    "They survived..."
    "What does it mean?"

Evanna stepped forward, her voice steady but kind. "The Queen is gone," she said, her words cutting through the murmurs. "The Court has been reborn. It's no longer a threat to us—it's a part of us."

The crowd was silent, their eyes wide with disbelief. An older man stepped forward, his weathered face lined with years of hardship. "And the shadows?" he asked, his voice trembling. "What of them?"

"They're still here," Evanna admitted. "But they're not the same. They're not enemies anymore. They're part of the balance—the dusk that protects us from chaos."

The man frowned, his gaze skeptical. "And how can we trust that balance won't tip again?"

Callen stepped beside Evanna, his voice firm. "Because we won't let it. The Court has new guardians now—people who will protect it and ensure it serves the Vale, not its own desires."

The villagers exchanged uncertain glances, but a spark of hope began to flicker in their eyes. Slowly, they nodded, their fear giving way to cautious optimism.

—-

As the days turned into weeks, Evanna and Callen worked tirelessly to rebuild the Vale. They traveled from village to village, sharing the truth of what had happened and listening to the fears and concerns of the people. It was not an easy task—many still harbored deep distrust of the Court and its power—but Evanna's compassion and Callen's unwavering resolve began to win them over.

The Court itself had become a symbol of change, its transformation visible even from a distance. Its spires no longer loomed like dark sentinels; instead, they reached toward the sky with a quiet grace, their surfaces shimmering faintly in the eternal dusk. The shadows that had once spilled from its gates now lingered quietly within, their presence more like that of watchful guardians than oppressive invaders.

—-

One evening, as Evanna and Callen returned to the Court after another long journey through the Vale, they were met by a strange sight. A group of villagers had gathered at the base of the Court's steps, their faces a mix of awe and trepidation. At their center stood a young girl, her hands clasped around a bundle of flowers.

"What's going on?" Evanna asked as she approached, her curiosity piqued.

The girl stepped forward hesitantly, her eyes wide as she looked up at Evanna and Callen. "We wanted to thank you," she said softly, her voice barely above a whisper. "For protecting us. For saving the Vale."

Evanna's heart swelled with emotion as she knelt before the girl, accepting the flowers with a grateful smile. "Thank you," she said, her voice gentle. "But this isn't just our victory—it's yours too. The Vale belongs to all of us."

The villagers murmured in agreement, their expressions softening. They began to place offerings at the foot of the steps—small tokens of gratitude, from candles and food to handmade trinkets. The sight filled Evanna with a deep sense of purpose, a reminder of why they had fought so hard to protect the Vale.

—-

As night fell, Evanna and Callen stood at the top of the Court's steps, looking out over the gathering below. The eternal dusk bathed the land in its soft, golden light, casting long shadows that danced gently in the breeze. For the first time in what felt like forever, Evanna felt a sense of peace.

"Do you think we can really do this?" she asked, her voice quiet but steady.

Callen turned to her, his expression thoughtful. "It won't be easy," he said. "There's still so much we don't know about the Court—about the balance we're supposed to protect. But I think... as long as we stay together, we can figure it out."

Evanna nodded, her gaze distant as she thought of the boy and the promise they had made to honor his sacrifice. "He trusted us with this," she said. "We can't let him down."

"We won't," Callen said firmly. "We'll make sure the Court becomes what it was always meant to be—a place of balance, not fear."

—-

As the days turned into months, the Vale began to heal. The people grew accustomed to the new presence of the Court, and the shadows, once feared and hated, became a quiet part of their lives. Evanna and Callen continued to serve as guardians, their bond strengthening with each challenge they faced together.

But the dusk remained eternal, a constant reminder of the delicate balance they had sworn to protect. It was neither day nor night, neither light nor dark—a space in between, fragile yet resilient.

And though the shadows lingered, they were no longer a threat. They were a promise.

A reminder that even in the darkest places, there could be light.

And so, the Vale stood, a kingdom reborn under the soft glow of the eternal dusk, its people united by the sacrifices that had shaped their world. Evanna and Callen watched over it, not as rulers, but as protectors.

For they had learned that true strength lay not in power, but in love, sacrifice, and the unyielding determination to hold the balance.

The Court of Endless Dusk would endure, its story written not in fear, but in hope. And with every passing moment, the Vale whispered its promise: that even in the face of darkness, there would always be light.

155